DATE DUE			

Working but Poo

Working but Poor

America's Contradiction

Revised Edition

Sar A. Levitan, Frank Gallo,
and Isaac Shapiro

The Johns Hopkins University Press   Baltimore and London

Printed in the United States of America
Originally published, hardcover and paperback, 1987
Revised edition, 1993

The Johns Hopkins University Press
2715 North Charles Street
Baltimore, Maryland 21218-4319
The Johns Hopkins Press Ltd., London

Levitan, Sar A.
    Working but poor : America's contradiction / Sar A. Levitan, Frank
Gallo, and Isaac Shapiro. — Rev. ed.
    p. cm.
    Includes bibliographical references and index.
    ISBN 0-8018-4574-2 (hc). — ISBN 0-8018-4575-0 (pbk)
    1. Income maintenance programs—United States. 2. Poor—
Employment—United States. 3. Manpower policy—United States.
4. Working class—United States. 5. Wages—United States.
6. United States—Economic conditions—1981–   7. United States—
Social conditions—1980–   I. Gallo, Frank. II. Shapiro, Isaac.
1957– . III. Title.
HC110.I5L468   1993
362.5′0973—dc20   92-34719

A catalog record for this book is available from the British Library

Contents

Preface to the Revised Edition

This book is a completely revised edition of a volume published six years ago, reissued because of growing public interest in the interrelationship between work and poverty. Revitalized government awareness of the importance of antipoverty measures that promote work has led to the enactment of several important reforms since the first edition appeared. These include significant expansions of the earned income tax credit, work-related programs for welfare recipients, child care assistance, and adult education. The revised volume also includes greater attention to the impact of eroding family structure on the working poor, the necessity for individual rectitude in avoiding or escaping poverty, and the effect of government policies on work incentives. Finally, computer advances have enabled analysts to better use survey data to more thoroughly explore problems and programs related to work and poverty. Access to previously unavailable information has allowed the authors to improve the book.

This study examines the experiences and hardships encountered by poor workers, and it assesses how well government policies ameliorate deprivation and enable or encourage work. Contrary to the widespread perception that poverty is due to indolence, 2 million people work full-time, year-round but remain poor, and nearly another 7 million poor individuals work full-time for part of the year or in part-time jobs.

Working but Poor profiles poor workers, examines the severity of their income problems, and analyzes the nature of low-wage job markets, including unemployment, technological developments, immigration, and international trade. The impact of household structure and size upon poverty among workers is also assessed. No single problem explains the glaring contradiction of poverty among workers amidst an affluent economy, although declining earnings and the growth of single-parent families have been among the most deleterious developments in recent years.

This volume emphasizes the role and responsibility of the government in alleviating the problems of poor workers, but also stresses the necessity of effort and rectitude among the impoverished. Recognizing that different strategies are necessary to address the problems and needs of poor workers, this study assesses four separate but related government efforts:

Minimum-wage and tax policies that bolster the income from work;

Policies that remove employment obstacles by promoting education and job training, equal employment opportunity, and child care. These policies help the poor to find work and aid the upward mobility of those already employed;

Policies that help the employable but idle poor find jobs by matching the unemployed with job openings, providing incentives to employers for hiring the poor, or directly creating jobs; and

Income assistance and in-kind benefit policies that supplement the incomes of workers whose wages do not allow them to escape poverty.

Government policies assisting poor workers have never been generous, although since the mid-1980s both poverty debates and legislative reforms have demonstrated a greater concern with encouraging work. Aiding poor workers embodies the principles of an affluent and just society that promotes economic opportunity.

The final chapter recommends a modified government agenda that would more vigorously assist poor workers. Government policy should assist workers to secure sufficient earnings to escape poverty, as well as to enable or encourage work among the able-bodied, nonworking poor. The proposed reforms would be implemented over several years, and include raising the minimum wage, expanding the earned income tax credit, creating jobs for both the working and nonworking poor, expanding affordable child care, boosting funding for education and job training, ensuring access to affordable health insurance, and reinvigorating enforcement of equal employment opportunity. Although the necessary outlays are considerable, the price for failing to help the working poor escape poverty may be even higher in the long run.

To avoid excessive footnotes, we have not cited material from routine annual government publications, or unpublished government data. Most of the uncited information in this book emanates from two sources: regularly published government reports from the U.S. Census Bureau and Bureau of Labor Statistics, or unpublished data generated in the preparations of these reports; and the annual *Green Book,* produced by the U.S. House Committee on Ways and Means, which has truly become an authoritative and comprehensive source on federal social programs.

The study was supported by an ongoing grant from the Ford Foundation to the Center for Social Policy Studies at the George Washington University. In line with the foundation's practice, responsibility for the contents of the study was left with the center director.

Acknowledgments

The unstinting help of numerous U.S. government analysts made this book possible, especially those in the Census Bureau, Bureau of Labor Statistics, Education Department, Congressional Research Service, General Accounting Office, and Congressional Budget Office. We would like to particularly thank Andrew Sum, Neal Fogg, and the rest of the staff at the Northeastern University Center for Labor Market Studies, who shared their voluminous tabulations from the Census Bureau's Current Population Survey. The center has become an important resource on issues related to family, work, and poverty through its thorough mining of social and economic surveys. Enrique Lamas of the U.S. Census Bureau was instrumental in providing us with data generated from a special project on the receipt of government benefits. Robert Greenstein and Jerry McBride of the Center on Budget and Policy Priorities provided help on several chapters. Finally, we are indebted to Miriam Washington for preparing the volume for publication and Elizabeth Miller for composing the figures.

1

The Concurrence of Work and Poverty

1. The Working Poor in an Affluent Nation

The working poor remain America's glaring contradiction. The concurrence of work and poverty is contrary to the American ethos that a willingness to work leads to material advancement, and it negates the prevalent view that the cause of poverty among adults capable of work is deviant behavior, particularly a lack of commitment to work.

The working poor are not an isolated few. In 1991, 2 million adults—59 percent more than in 1978—worked full-time throughout the year, yet they and their families remained poor. Another 7.2 million poor individuals worked either in full-time jobs for part of the year or in part-time jobs. Because of limited job opportunities, inadequate skills, and the low wages prevailing in some occupations or geographic areas, they continue to have low earnings.

The American economic and political system has produced vigorous economic progress, facilitating upward mobility. Millions moved out of poverty into the middle and upper classes, and the number of poor workers continued to decline until the 1970s. Individuals who fail to apply themselves are likely to be impoverished, and poverty, conversely, can breed dysfunctional behavior. Greater commitment to work and skill training can rightly be expected among many of the able-bodied poor. But blind faith in the free market system and a blanket indictment of the poor are unwarranted. The difficult living conditions of poor workers and the complex factors that account for their existence should not be

Figure 1. The number of poor workers has risen since the 1970s.

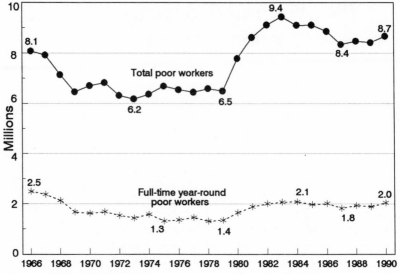

Source: U.S. Census Bureau

ignored. Government intervention is essential to improve their lives and prospects.

The Problem

After a sharp decline in the number of poor workers in the late 1960s, the level, though fluctuating with economic conditions, remained relatively stable until 1978, before rising sharply from 1979 to 1983. (Figure 1). The subsequent economic recovery reduced the working poor by 700,000, but the number climbed again as a result of the recent recession.

These data are based on the federal government's official poverty thresholds. Despite conceptual and technical measurement problems, the government's poverty index has gained wide acceptance. Each year the thresholds are adjusted to reflect changes in the level of consumer prices. The poverty thresholds are adjusted for family size and the age of the household head. The estimated 1992 thresholds for nonelderly households were:

Number of individuals in household	Poverty threshold
One	$ 7,320
Two	9,467
Three	11,216
Four	14,381
Five	17,000
Six	19,204
Seven	21,790
Eight	24,310
Nine or more	28,902

Most poor workers are white, as are a majority of all individuals in poverty. Three-fifths of the poor who work full-time, year-round are men; women constitute a similar majority of the poor who work full-time for part of the year or who work part-time. The working poor have a better chance of escaping poverty than the nonworking poor, but their income and employment problems are often persistent, partly because they often possess limited skills.

To visualize the deprivation of the poor, imagine what it would be like to live on income equal to the poverty line. The poverty threshold is based on the assumptions that a third of income is spent on food; in 1992 this fraction was equivalent to a little more than $1 per meal per person. The financial complaints of many middle-income families earning two or three times the poverty line is another vivid sign of the difficult circumstances of the working poor. A third of poor workers aged 16 to 64 have family incomes below half the poverty line; they find it even tougher to meet their basic food, shelter, and medical needs.

In a nation as affluent as the United States, the existence of numerous impoverished workers is disturbing. It raises serious questions about the fairness of income distribution. It challenges our faith in the American Dream: that those who work hard prosper. It is difficult and, indeed, inaccurate to believe in this dream when millions who work remain poor. Many of these jobs are dead ends, not stepping stones to opportunity.

When work brings few material rewards and upward mobility is unattainable, commitment to work is easily undermined, and alienation is inevitable. There is clearly a need to reconsider the impact of market wages and welfare upon incentives to work. But the current debate emphasizes the work disincentives of welfare, while ignoring the limited incentives that labor bestows upon poor workers.

An economic system best promotes the work ethic when labor is sufficiently rewarded. Public policy should not only assist welfare recipients to attain economic self-sufficiency but also aid those who work but remain poor. Government policies that help lift workers and their families from impoverishment not only benefit the individuals directly affected, they also send a message to non-workers that labor provides a route out of poverty. A society that glorifies the work ethic should reward those who practice it.

The lessons to be drawn from an analysis of the working poor apply to a much larger group of workers. Millions of individuals work in low-wage jobs but have other sources of income (often from family members) that lift them above the poverty threshold. In 1990 almost one out of ten workers employed full-time, year-round did not earn enough to raise a family of three above the poverty threshold. Many low-wage workers will also benefit from higher minimum wages and other federal policies that help poor workers.

The Job Market for Low-Wage Workers

The number of poor workers reflects economic and demographic trends, individual behavior, and the effectiveness of government policies. In depressed economic conditions, low-wage workers are bound to experience difficulties. Not only are they more likely to be forced into unemployment or part-time work, but their already low wages are likely to stagnate or decline. Opportunities for upward mobility, through raises or new jobs, are reduced. But even during recovery periods, increasing international competition has contributed to a weak demand for workers, causing job losses and wage cutbacks. Federal economic policies have not addressed either problem effectively. Macroeconomic policy has generally focused on lowering inflation—even when it resulted in higher unemployment—and direct government action to aid the working poor remains inadequate.

Pockets of economic dislocation, moreover, are partially insulated from national economic growth. The working poor tend to be concentrated in troubled local economies and in a few occupations and industries, including low-skilled blue-collar, service, and agricultural employment. Many of their jobs are in the "secondary labor market," which is characterized by high turnover, few worker protections, limited training, and little opportunity for upward mobility. Secondary labor market workers lack clout on the job and are heavily dependent on government to improve their employment conditions.

The number of poor workers also reflects population trends. A large supply of low-wage workers can slow wage growth. Illegal immigrants are in no position to challenge inadequate wages and other working conditions imposed by employers. In the 1960s and 1970s more immigrants, women, and youth entered the labor market, but in an expanding economy these workers were absorbed, and the number of poor workers tended to decline. Subsequent population trends have been mixed: immigrants, both legal and illegal, continue to enter the work force in large numbers, but the number of youth entrants declined sharply. Young female work-force entrants now match men in educational attainment, and therefore they are not much more likely than men to become impoverished workers unless they are single parents.

Federal Policies

The federal government influences the fate of poor workers not only through broad macroeconomic and trade policies, but also through a wide variety of more targeted policies. These policies specifically affect worker compensation and help break down skill and other barriers to employment. They also help the poor secure employment and supplement their income through welfare and social insurance.

Federal minimum-wage and tax policies have a direct impact on the compensation of low-wage employees. Established in 1938 as part of the Fair Labor Standards Act, the minimum wage places a floor under wages, which helps to ensure minimally acceptable living standards. The coverage and value of the minimum wage expanded until the 1980s.

Because of inflation the worth of the federal minimum wage fell dramatically in the 1980s, reducing the earnings of millions of workers, many of whom were poor. By 1989 the purchasing power of the minimum wage was at its lowest level since the 1940s. The increases in 1990 and 1991 from \$3.35 to \$4.25 per hour fell well short of restoring the purchasing power lost because of inflation. By 1992 the earnings of a full-time, year-round minimum-wage worker were less than four-fifths of the poverty line for a three-person family. In contrast, throughout most of the 1960s and 1970s, full-time work at the minimum wage lifted a family of three above the poverty threshold. Exemptions from coverage and weak enforcement have allowed employers to pay many workers less than the federal minimum, further undermining the effectiveness of the standard.

While the value of the minimum wage declined during the first half of the 1980s, taxation on poor workers rose. Federal taxes for a two-parent family of four living at the poverty threshold jumped from 1.8 percent of income in 1979 to 10.4 percent in 1985. The 1986 tax law reduced the tax burden of the poor to the levels of the late 1970s. The law exempted more income from taxation and raised the earned income tax credit, which offsets social security taxes for low earners with dependents. These tax provisions are indexed to inflation and will free working-poor families with children from onerous federal taxes for the foreseeable future. Congress expanded the earned income tax credit further in 1990, but this did not fully offset the decline in the value of the minimum wage.

Skill deficiencies impede gainful employment for many poor Americans. About one in four working-age poor individuals is functionally illiterate. Nearly two in five poor workers lack a high school diploma, and one in nine has a work disability. Federal second-chance programs assist those who did not acquire adequate basic skills prior to entering the work force.

Adult education programs teach literacy or numeracy, help enrollees attain diplomas and certificates, or prepare participants for vocational training. Rehabilitation programs train or provide other work-related help to the disabled. The Job Training Partnership Act (JTPA) trains economically disadvantaged youth and adults. The Job Corps, a part of JTPA, provides comprehensive skill training in a residential setting for severely disadvantaged youth. Second-chance programs have always been underfunded relative to the number of individuals who lack salable basic skills. This disparity has widened since the early 1980s, when the federal government cut inflation-adjusted funding for employment and training efforts by two-thirds, to a level where it remained in 1992.

Some low-wage workers with adequate skills cannot obtain higher-paying jobs because of other employment barriers. Spurred by the civil and women's rights movements, federal antidiscrimination policies have opened employment opportunities to women and minorities since the mid-1960s. However, weak enforcement of antidiscrimination laws hampers continued progress in the workplace for women and minorities.

Poor parents often cannot secure full- or even part-time employment because they lack adequate, affordable childcare. This problem is particularly acute for the rising number of poor single-parent families. The federal government either directly or indirectly subsidizes some childcare through Head Start, the social-services block-grant program, the Family Support Act, and other childcare programs. If adequate, low-cost care was more readily available, the poor could work more, and their children's lives would improve. In recent years, governments at all levels have expanded support of childcare for the employable poor, but much more remains to be done.

The federal-state employment service, which matches workers with job openings, attempts to facilitate the functioning of the low-wage labor market. When the job-matching process is expedited, unemployment is reduced. The employment service helps fill millions of jobs each year, but in the last decade its funding has been reduced, and low-income individuals constitute a much smaller share of its clientele.

The targeted jobs tax credit provides a tax credit to employers who hire disadvantaged low-wage workers. The credit is intended to encourage employers to hire workers, particularly poor youth and welfare recipients, who because of limited skills or other employment barriers have trouble breaking into the job market. However, there is considerable evidence that the act frequently subsidizes the employment of workers who would have been hired even if this program did not exist.

The federal government has also periodically funded jobs for the unemployed. A major jobs program enacted in the 1970s was eliminated in 1981, thus depriving the government of a vital tool to help the unemployed and welfare recipients who seek self-sufficiency. Funding continues for smaller jobs programs that primarily assist youth and the elderly.

In sum, the severe reduction of federal employment and training programs has curtailed job opportunities for the working and nonworking poor. The retrenchment has taken place even though funding of federal second-chance programs has always been meager.

Federal policies that make work pay and enhance employment opportunities reduce the need to support the able-bodied poor. But in part because federal policies do not sufficiently promote upward mobility, millions of able bodied individuals require welfare as a last resort. If these workers are to escape poverty, their earnings must be supplemented by welfare.

The complex federal income security system includes cash assistance, in-kind benefits, and social insurance programs. The extent of government support provided to poor workers varies sharply. Aid to Families with Dependent Children (AFDC), the primary means-tested cash-assistance program, has always been of moderate assistance to working families. In 1990 only 8 percent of AFDC families reported any earnings, compared with 13 percent in 1979. Federal in-kind benefit programs include food stamps, Medicaid, and public housing assistance. Funding for in-kind programs exceeds cash welfare outlays, but only a minority of poor workers benefit from these programs. Social insurance programs, including social security and unemployment insurance, extend benefits to recipients of all income levels. These programs greatly help the poor, but usually not when they are working.

The 1988 Family Support Act included several measures to facilitate AFDC recipients' transition to self-sufficiency. The law mandates that states provide childcare to individuals who enroll in education, employment, or training programs. Individuals who leave the welfare rolls due to work retain entitlement for childcare and health-care services for as long as one year. Since 1989, appropriations designed to assist welfare recipients to attain self-sufficiency have increased, but welfare-to-work expenditures remain below the peak level attained during the 1970s. Current funding is adequate to assist only a small fraction of employable AFDC recipients, and the program includes no subsidized employment component for graduates unable to secure jobs.

The Future

Throughout much of the 1960s and 1970s, the federal government substantially assisted the working poor. Macroeconomic policies sought to minimize overall unemployment, and job training and job creation efforts were expanded. The minimum wage provided a reasonable wage floor, and the federal government introduced new initiatives such as equal employment opportunity laws. Welfare and social insurance programs were generally strengthened. These efforts bolstered economic security.

Subsequent federal policy changes have reduced assistance to poor workers and relaxed enforcement of existing protections. Opposition to antipoverty programs remains strong, and the troublesome budget deficit as well as projected slow economic growth make it unlikely that the federal government will commit substantial additional resources to assisting poor workers. There are few signs that wage rates will rise significantly.

The outlook for the working poor, however, is not completely dismal. The retrenchments left the policy framework largely intact. Some programs in aid of poor workers can be strengthened without raising the federal deficit. Restoring the minimum wage to its traditional level, for example, will not raise federal expenditures, nor will vigorous enforcement of equal employment opportunity laws. Other programs, particularly job creation, training, and placement policies, require larger up-front investments but in the long run some of these funds are recouped through increased tax revenues and a drop in welfare costs. Promoting gainful employment is ultimately a cost-effective investment for the federal government and society as a whole. Most important, it helps the poor attain more rewarding lives.

Future progress in aiding poor workers and promoting labor among the nonworking but able-bodied poor depends largely on the nation's political will. Several recent reforms indicate that the connection between work and poverty is becoming more widely recognized. Poor workers have benefited from the expansion of the earned income tax credit, childcare assistance, work-welfare initiatives, literacy programs, and a partial restoration of the value of the minimum wage. Efforts that help individuals work their way out of poverty and off welfare can balance the goals of economic support and economic self-sufficiency. In addition, they support the underlying premise and promise of the work ethic. The public is especially supportive of programs that promote upward economic mobility among the poor who are trying to help themselves.

2

The Setting

2. Profile of the Working Poor

The working poor account for a small fraction of the employed. In 1991 some 2.6 percent of all full-time, year-round workers were poor, and 7.0 percent of those with any work experience lived in poverty. Employment enables most workers to escape impoverishment.

In absolute numbers and as a share of the poverty population, however, the working poor constitute a disturbing social problem. Nearly 9.3 million workers remained poor in 1991, 2 million of whom worked full-time, year-round. Many more poor people lived in families with at least one worker. Altogether, nearly three-fifths of the poor lived in households where someone worked during the year. The proportion rises to two-thirds for poor families with children. In 1990, 21.8 million people lived in poor families with children. Of these, 14.5 million lived in families with a worker, and 5.5 million people lived in poor families with children that had at least one full-time, year-round worker.

The majority of working poor families had workers employed for a substantial part of the year. In 1989, when the number of hours worked by all family members is combined, seven in ten working poor families with children were employed for the equivalent of five or more months of full-time work.[1] As further evidence of the work effort among many poor families, some families remain poor even though more than one of its members is employed. In 1990, 1 million of the 5.6 million poor families with children had two or more workers.

Figure 2. The poverty rate has increased slightly compared with the latter half of the 1970s.

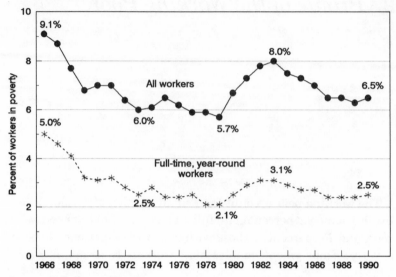

Source: U.S. Census Bureau

Earnings constitute a significant source of income for the poor. In 1990 earnings accounted for 63 percent of the money income of impoverished two-parent families with children and 37 percent of impoverished female-headed families. Among poor individuals under age 65 who live alone, earnings constituted 48 percent of income.

More Workers Are Falling into Poverty

During the past decade, the percentage of workers who fell into poverty was somewhat higher than in the latter half of the 1970s (Figure 2). A comparison of 1979 and 1989—both final years of long economic recoveries and therefore comparable years in the economic cycle—helps illustrate this point. In 1989, 6.3 percent of all workers were poor, rising from 5.7 percent in 1979. Similarly, in 1989, 2.4 percent of full-time workers were poor, up from 2.1 percent in 1979.

The increased incidence of poverty among workers, combined

with population growth, significantly augmented the overall number of poor workers. From 1979 to 1989, the number of full-time, year-round poor workers rose by 38 percent, from 1,365,000 to 1,887,000, and rose to 2,038,000 in 1990 as a result of a recession that began in mid-year. The number of partially working poor rose 26 percent from 1979 to 1989, and 30 percent from 1979 to 1990. Although data for 1991 were not available by mid-1992, the 1990–91 recession and the slow recovery have most likely exacerbated the problems of the working poor.

These trends sharply contrast with the experience of the 1960s and 1970s. Both the number of poor workers and the percentage of workers who were poor fell sharply during the 1960s before the number stabilized in the 1970s, while the percentage dropped somewhat. This progress was reversed from 1979 to 1983, when the number and percentage of working poor rose dramatically as a consequence of back-to-back recessions and inflation before declining in the subsequent economic recovery.

The rise in the number of working poor parallels other economic trends, including growing income disparities in the United States. While those with low after-tax incomes have lost ground, the after-tax incomes of those in the middle have stagnated, and the after-tax incomes of the wealthy have risen dramatically (Figure 3).

In 1990, *before*-tax income was more unevenly divided than at any time since the end of World War II, except for 1989. Since the end of the 1960s, the share of pre-tax income held by the poorest population quintile generally has fallen, while the share held by the wealthiest fifth has risen. By contrast, the distribution of income had generally become more equal from the end of the 1940s to the end of the 1960s. The recent growth in income disparities suggests the need for policies aimed at achieving economic growth that is more broadly shared among the population.

	Share of national before-tax income		
	1970	*1980*	*1990*
Poorest fifth	5.4%	5.1%	4.6%
Broad middle	53.6	53.4	51.2
Richest fifth	40.9	41.6	44.3

(Numbers do not total to 100% due to rounding.)

Figure 3. After-tax incomes of the lowest two quintiles declined between 1977 and 1989.

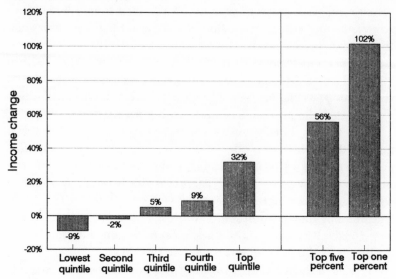

Source: U.S. Congressional Budget Office

Slightly More of the Poor Are Working

The 1960s were characterized by rising real wages and, to some degree, expanding government programs. As a result, many previously poor workers were able to earn their way out of poverty. From 1966 until 1975, the proportion of poor adults (those aged 16 or older) who worked full-time, year-round fell nearly in half. The direction of the trend altered in the late 1970s. By 1989 the proportion of poor adults who worked, as well as the proportion who worked full-time, year-round, was up slightly from 1979.

The likelihood of poor families with children having someone working at all was similar in 1979 and 1989, but the average time spent working increased slightly. This increase occurred among both poor married-couple families and poor female-headed families. The major factor that accounts for the relative unresponsiveness of poverty to economic growth in the 1980s, as contrasted with the sharp fall in poverty during the 1960s, was the decline in real wages during the latter decade.[2] The unresponsiveness was not due to a decline in work effort.

Table 1. Characteristics of the working poor compared with all workers (1990)

	All workers	All working poor	Part-time working poor	Full-time, year-round working poor
Race				
White	86%	74%	74%	74%
Nonwhite	14	26	26	26
Sex				
Male	54	47	43	60
Female	46	53	57	40
Age				
16–17 years	2	4	5	0.4
18–24 years	15	26	29	15
25–64 years	79	68	64	83
65 years or older	4	2	2	1

Source: U.S. Census Bureau

Characteristics

The vast majority of the working poor are white and a similarly large majority are aged 25 to 64, but the working poor are less likely to be white or of prime working age than all workers (Table 1). The full-time, year-round working poor include more men than women, while the partially working poor include more women than men. Childcare responsibilities often limit women to part-time work. More than half of poor workers—56 percent—live in families with children. A little less than a third—31 percent—live alone. The remainder live in childless families.

The working poor are overrepresented in nonmetropolitan areas and tend to be concentrated in "poverty areas" in which 20 percent or more of the population is below the poverty level. In 1987 (latest available data), 41 percent of working poor householders lived in poverty areas, compared to only 15 percent of all householders. Overall growth in the U.S. economy may not be of much help to individuals trapped in these pockets of poverty.

Serious educational and skill deficiencies contribute to the employment problems of poor workers: 40 percent have not graduated from high school. Skill training programs, especially those that emphasize basic competency, are essential to alleviate the problems experienced by the working poor. In addition, physical or mental disabilities afflict 5 percent of the full-time, year-round working poor and 13 percent of the partially working poor. The working poor are employed in a surprisingly wide range of occupations, although they are overrepresented in service, low-skilled blue-collar and agricultural jobs. A lack of skills consigns some individuals to low-paying jobs, while the unavailability of higher-paying positions due to either discrimination or insufficient demand keeps some skilled workers in poverty.

Why Don't Many of the Poor Work?

In 1990 one of every two individuals aged 16 to 64 who lived in poverty worked at least part of the year, compared with 84 percent of the nonpoor. Nearly three of every five poor male working-age adults had some work experience during the year, compared to four in ten poor females. Slightly more than half of impoverished white adults and two of every five impoverished black adults had some work experience during the year. These differences in work effort are explained in part by the parental responsibilities of women and by the greater difficulty experienced by women and blacks in finding jobs.

	Distribution (1990)	
	Nonpoor	*Poor*
Total, aged 16 to 64 (millions)	142.6	17.6
Percentage	100%	100%
Worked	84	48
Full-time year-round	54	11
Less than full-time	30	37
Did not work	16	52

Poor adults work much less than adults who are not poor. One explanation lies in a lack of effort by the poor. An alternative explanation is that lack of opportunities and other constraints combine to prevent many of the poor from holding jobs that would provide them with earnings sufficient to escape poverty. Although

Figure 4. In 1990 the poor aged 16 to 64 years were more likely than the nonpoor to be ill or disabled or unable to find work.

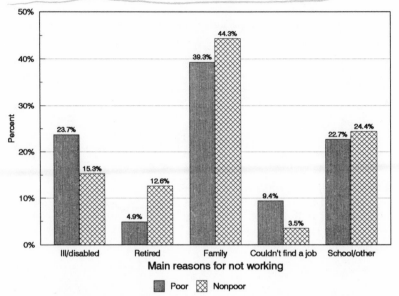

Source: U.S. Census Bureau

greater effort should be expected from many poor adults, the second explanation applies to most poor adults.

The inability of some individuals to find work is verified by the fact that those in poverty claiming to be unemployed drops sharply in periods of economic growth. In addition, the number of people seeking work far exceeds the number of job vacancies, even during boom times.

Family responsibilities are the single most common reason offered by the poor for not working, although a disproportionately large share of the nonelderly poor do not work because of health problems or an inability to find work (Figure 4). Because the majority of all women with children under six years old are currently in the labor force, "keeping house" typically is an insufficient reason for not working. However, affordable childcare is often not available for the poor, and working full-time may not be a viable alternative for a significant proportion of mothers with young children.

Table 2. More than three-fifths of poor workers live in families headed by single women or men, or outside of families altogether (1990)

	Distribution		
	---	---	---
Household status	*All workers*	*Poor workers*	*Poverty rate*
All 16- to 64-year-olds	127.7 million	8.5 million	6.7%
Families			
Married couples	68.0%	36.2%	3.5
Female heads	10.6	27.1	17.1
Male heads	3.4	3.5	6.9
Nonfamilies			
Unrelated subfamilies	0.4	2.4	37.4
Unrelated individuals	17.6	30.8	11.7

Source: U.S. Census Bureau

Family Matters

The erosion of family structure has made the problems of poor workers much more intractable in recent decades. Unmarried family heads constitute an increasing share of working poor families. The earning potential of these families is distinctly limited, and the presence of children further restricts potential work time. The fact that the earnings of women still trail behind those of men further limits their income. Also, working poor families are larger than those of the working nonpoor, which increases the amount of income needed to escape poverty. Unlike nonpoor workers, most poor earners do not live in a married-couple family (Table 2). More than half of black poor workers live in families headed by a single parent.

The Rise in Female-Headed Families

In the early 1960s most working poor families were married couples with a nonworking wife. But because many married-couple families were able to work their way out of poverty and because of the increase in single-parent families, nearly half of working poor families are now headed by a single woman. Most of this shift occurred between 1959 and 1979:

1959	16.8%
1969	31.3
1979	41.3
1990	45.5

In 1990 the average number of workers per poor family was 1.4 workers. This number differed little between married couples and female-headed families, although the latter was more likely to contain children.

Poverty rates among workers did not increase by household type during the 1980s, except among married-couple families. Apparently family factors contributed to the overall rise in poverty because of the greater likelihood that workers lived in single-parent families.

	Poverty rate	
Workers aged 16 to 64 by household type	1979	1989
Total	5.8%	6.4%
Married-couple families	3.2	3.5
Female-headed families	16.1	16.2
Unrelated individuals	11.9	11.5

The total annual work time among working poor families also changed little. Low wages and limited work time combine to make the annual earnings of working-poor households disturbingly low, with unrelated individuals faring the worst.

Annual earnings of poor workers (1990)		
Household type	Per family	Per worker
All families	$5,871	$4,350
Married couples	7,343	4,918
Female-headed	4,373	3,625
Unrelated individuals	—	2,990

Another factor suggests that the heaviest burden of poverty falls upon female-headed working-poor households. One-fourth of working-poor, married-couple family heads were self-employed in 1987, compared to 5 percent of female-headed householders and

11 percent of unrelated individuals. Poverty among the self-employed may reflect a bad business year rather than a persistent problem. Moreover, under-reporting of self-employed income is a significant problem in economic surveys, and thus the poverty of some of these workers is no more than a statistical artifact.

In poor families a working household head contributes about 90 percent of total family earnings, even when other family members work.[3] In 1990 in married-couple working-poor families almost half of the wives worked, compared to 85 percent of the husbands.

Poverty and Family Size

The average working-poor family supports half a person more than the average working-nonpoor family (3.8 vs. 3.3 members). Compared with whites, blacks and Hispanics have larger families and lower earnings. Poor black workers face an additional handicap because more than half of them live in female-headed families, compared with one-fifth of poor Hispanic workers. The average minority working-poor family supports one family member more than the average white working-nonpoor family:

Average family size of working families (1990)

Race/ethnicity	Married couple		Female-headed	
	Nonpoor	Poor	Nonpoor	Poor
Total	4.1	4.7	3.1	3.8
White	4.1	4.6	2.9	3.1
Black	4.3	5.0	3.5	3.9
Hispanic	4.5	5.0	3.5	3.9

The additional income needed to raise larger families to the poverty threshold is roughly one-fourth of the average annual earnings of working-poor two-parent families, and one-sixth of comparable earnings for single mothers. The difference in family size between poor minority and nonpoor white married couples necessitates an extra $2,000 for the former to raise their families to the poverty line. Caring for children also limits potential paid work time, and it may necessitate additional childcare expenses for working parents. Some 56 percent of poor workers have children younger than 18 years. There is a close relationship between family size and poverty.

Working families	*Poverty rate (1987)*
Total	6.7%
Number of children	
none	2.7
one	7.3
two	8.1
three or more	18.4

The combination of single-parent families, family size, and falling earnings among young workers has led to greater increases in poverty among young working parents during the past decade.

Poverty rates of families with working heads		
Family type	*1979*	*1990*
Family head younger than age 30	9.0%	15.4%
Without children	2.9	2.9
With children	12.3	22.2
Family head age 30 to 64	4.8	5.4

In 1990 one of every four poor working parents was aged 16 to 24, and more than half of these young parents had at least two children.

Clearly, family size is a major factor in determining whether family income falls below the poverty threshold. The birth of a child may cause parents to fall into poverty and make it much harder for them to climb out. It has always been extremely difficult for a single parent to finance a family, and the increasing number of such families has made them a large and growing proportion of the working poor. The disturbing increase in out-of-wedlock births, which accounted for 27 percent of all births in 1989 and shows no signs of slowing, has particularly exacerbated the poverty problem because never-married mothers tend to be deficiently educated and therefore unlikely to command sufficient earnings to escape poverty. Efforts to obtain child support from absent fathers have intensified in recent years, and the pressure should be further increased. But since poor women tend to become involved with poor men, preventive measures are more likely to be efficacious than child support.

The Extent of the Problem

The severity of the problems faced by the working poor is determined by how much help they receive from government benefits, as well as the duration of their poverty spells. Poor families with workers receive much less assistance from government benefit programs than poor families without workers. In 1990 the value of government cash and noncash transfers for poor nonelderly families with a full-time, year-round worker averaged $360, while for poor nonelderly families with a part-time worker these transfers averaged $2,280. In contrast, for poor nonelderly families without a worker, these transfers averaged $4,970.

The largest in-kind benefit programs for the poor are Medicaid, food stamps, and housing subsidies. In-kind benefit programs provide considerable assistance to the working poor. However, no more than two-fifths of working-poor households benefit from each of these programs. The usually cited "official" government statistics exclude the value of in-kind benefits, but about a fifth of the working poor would be lifted out of poverty if the value of these benefits was included.

Unreported income can lead to an overstatement of the poverty problem. Many of the working poor have expenditures that exceed their income in a particular year, in part because they are drawing down on assets or because they may be spending themselves into debt. On the other hand, the official poverty line may lead to the understatement of poverty. The poverty line was devised in 1965 and is based on the cost of an emergency food diet multiplied by three. Because housing and health-care prices rose more than the other components of the consumer price index, it would be more accurate if the multiplier were larger. More recent surveys of the amount of income required to meet current minimal needs also suggest the poverty line is too low.[4]

There is much mobility in and out of poverty, and the working poor are more likely to move off the poverty rolls than the nonworking poor. To analyze the duration of poverty for the working poor requires longitudinal studies that track the employment and income status of specific families and individuals over time. A small fraction of workers are poor in a particular year, and an even smaller fraction are persistently poor over time. Only 2.5

percent of the 119 million individuals who worked during both 1987 and 1988 were poor in both years.[5]

	Number (thousands)	Poverty rate
Worked in 1987 and 1988	118,960	NA
Poor in 1987	5,073	4.3%
Poor in 1988	4,613	3.9
Poor in either year	6,768	5.7
Poor in both years	2,918	2.5

Two-fifths of poor workers in 1987 escaped impoverishment the next year, a turnover rate roughly double that of nonelderly individuals who did not work in both years. Even though the working poor are more likely to escape poverty than the nonworking poor, not only did three-fifths of poor workers in 1987 remain poor in 1988, nearly half of poor workers who *did* escape poverty remained below 125 percent of the threshold.

Almost three in four poverty spells end due to an increase in earnings (as opposed to a rise in unearned income or a change in family status). The proportion is higher among male-headed families. At the same time, a drop in earnings explains about one-half of descents into poverty.[6] Only slightly more than a third of workers who descended into poverty in 1988 had incomes below 125 percent of the threshold in the year before. Evidence of upward mobility among the working poor should not obscure the serious labor-market and income problems that this group faces. More than any other indicator, the best predictor of future status in a low-wage job is whether a worker is currently in a low-wage job.[7]

A Chronic and Aggravated Problem

The problems of the working poor worsened somewhat in the 1980s. Although workers are more likely to be poor if they are minorities, women, or deficient in skills and education, most poor workers are white, half are men, some are skilled, and they are found in a wide range of occupations. The working poor receive less assistance from the government than the nonworking poor, but over time have a better chance of escaping poverty. Nevertheless, the income and labor-market problems of the working poor are often enduring.

3. Low-Wage Job Markets

Poor workers are highly concentrated in jobs that offer little opportunity for upward mobility and lack the protections common in better paid occupations. Low wages are only one of the labor-market problems common to the poor. Forced idleness, involuntary part-time employment, and a failure to seek work also cause poverty among workers.

The recent rise in the number of low-wage workers reflects the economy's lackluster performance and diminishing federal support. The growing numbers of single mothers and immigrants have also contributed to the rise of low-wage workers. Low-productivity growth and stagnating or declining wages since the early 1970s have particularly hurt low-wage workers. A booming economy would raise overall wage levels, but many of the working poor are concentrated in areas and jobs that too frequently do not benefit from overall economic growth.

Unemployment, Part-Time Employment, and Low Wages

Inadequate earnings reflect two work-related problems: low wages and/or insufficient hours, due to joblessness or part-time work. In addition, the size and total income of the household determine whether a low-wage earner is poor. In the absence of dependents, nearly half of the poor who worked full-time, year-round would not have been impoverished. On the other hand, the vast majority of low-wage workers are not poor, primarily because of the income of other household members.

As less than a quarter of the working poor labor full-time, year-round, insufficient hours of paid work is a major problem. Most joblessness or part-time work among the working poor is not attributable to unemployment or involuntary part-time work. The average poor worker was jobless for nearly five months in 1987 (the latest available data), but more than half of this jobless time was due to the worker being out of the labor force and not looking for work. Similarly, less than half of poor part-time workers in 1990 labored on a shorter schedule because they could not find a full-time job or because of slack business at a normally full-time position.

In 1990 a total of 3.8 million poor workers who labored for less than a full year offered the following reasons for failing to seek employment:

Home or family reasons	28.5%
Ill or disabled	14.0
Could not find work	10.0
Retired	2.3
School or other	45.2

A lack of affordable childcare combined with low wages means that for some working-poor families it makes more economic sense for one adult to mind the children than to take a paid job. Ill health or an inability to find work is largely outside an individual's control, and lost wages due to school attendance is usually a sensible trade-off for higher earnings in the long run. The exact share of poor workers who do not look for work during spells of joblessness because they are in school is unknown, but probably accounts for roughly a fifth of the total.

In 1990, 55 percent of poor workers experienced some part-time work. Unemployment and involuntary part-time employment cause considerable economic hardship to the working poor. Three-fifths of those who worked less than full-time, year-round were unemployed, worked involuntarily part-time, or both. Most unemployment and involuntary part-time employment is persistent. In 1990 nearly three-fifths of unemployment, and half of involuntary part-time employment, lasted more than three and a half months.

Total poor workers	*8.7 million*
Experienced forced idleness	
Unemployed but no involuntary part-time	19.8%
Both unemployed and involuntary part-time	13.2
Involuntary part-time but not unemployed	11.2
Did not experience forced idleness	
Full-time, year-round	23.5
Less than full-time, year-round	32.4

Many individuals who would be classified as poor based on their earnings alone are lifted above the poverty line by private unearned income or government cash transfers. In 1990 these factors were equally important in reducing the number of poor workers, but government transfers more effectively reduced the poverty gap—the difference between income and the poverty line.[1]

Poverty based on	*Poor workers (millions)*	*Poverty rate*	*Poverty gap*
Earnings only	15.3	11.5%	$4,155
Income minus government cash transfers	11.9	9.0	3,897
Official definition	8.7	6.5	3,326

Only 3 percent of poor workers earned more than $12,200 in 1990, slightly below the estimated poverty line for the average-size working-poor family of 3.8 members. The average working-poor family earned $5,900, and an unrelated individual earned half that amount. No more than one-sixth of workers facing a single employment impediment were poor (Table 3).

The poor work in most occupations, but in 1989 three-fifths held service, low-skilled blue-collar, or agricultural jobs (Table 4). Only one-third of all workers labored in these occupations.

The overall increase between 1979 and 1989 in the poverty rate among workers (5.7 to 6.3 percent) disproportionately affected low-skilled blue-collar and service workers. Although the share of low-skilled blue-collar workers in the total work force fell sig-

Table 3. Work experience, employment problems, and poverty (1990)

	Number (millions)	Poverty rate
Total workers	132.6	6.5%
Full-time, year-round	80.0	2.5
Worked less than full-time, year-round		
did not experience unemployment	34.7	10.9
experienced unemployment	17.9	16.0
Worked part-time at least one week	42.0	11.4
involuntary part-time work	2.1	16.6
Annual earnings less than $12,200	55.5	15.2
full-time, year-round workers	14.4	12.7

Sources: U.S. Bureau of Labor Statistics and U.S. Census Bureau

Table 4. Occupations of poor workers (1989)

Occupational group	All workers	Poor workers
Total (millions)	131.6	8.3
Service	14.2%	29.5%
Low-skilled blue-collar	15.4	22.2
Sales	12.5	12.4
Skilled blue-collar	11.4	9.9
Managerial, professional, and technical	27.7	8.9
Farming, forestry, and fishing	3.1	8.6
Administrative support	15.8	8.4

Source: Unpublished data from the 1990 Current Population Survey, supplied by Professor Andrew Sum, Northeastern University.

nificantly, their proportion among the working poor grew. Nearly one in six agricultural workers was poor. Somewhat surprisingly, only 3.4 percent of administrative-support workers, an occupation dominated by women, were poor. The poverty gap remained virtually unchanged at $3,500 (1992 dollars) in 1979 and 1989.

Troubling Earnings Trends

Earnings inequality has grown since the 1970s, with the bottom fifth of earners bearing the brunt of the burden.[2] The U.S. Census Bureau tracked low earnings trends for the past quarter of a century by examining inflation-adjusted earnings of less than $11,570 (1989 dollars), roughly equivalent to the poverty threshold for the average-sized working-poor family of 3.8 individuals. In the last two decades, the share of the work force consisting of low earners remained relatively constant, but only because of increased paid work time among women. The share of the overall work force that labored full-time, year-round rose from 56 to 61 percent in the decade after 1979. If more women had not worked full-time, their earnings would not have risen about the low-earnings threshold.

Inflation-adjusted hourly earnings have dropped. The proportion of full-time, year-round workers with earnings below the Census threshold declined sharply between 1964 and 1974, and remained largely unchanged between 1974 and 1979. Since 1979, however, the proportion has increased, reaching nearly one in five in 1990 (Figure 5). This increase affected all demographic categories. Between 1964 and 1979, due to earnings growth and smaller households, the poverty rate among all low earners dropped by nearly half, before climbing during the next decade. However, poverty rates continued to fall among full-time, year-round low earners.[3]

Proportion with low earnings	1964	1969	1979	1989	1990
All workers	48.4%	42.3%	40.1%	40.4%	41.9%
Full-time, year-round workers	24.1	14.4	12.1	16.3	18.0
Poverty rate among low earners					
All workers	24.3	15.1	13.7	15.1	15.2
Full-time, year-round workers	26.9	18.6	15.5	12.5	12.7

Growing earnings inequity is attributable to a variety of factors, including greater employer demand for college-educated workers, the fall in the value of the minimum wage, international trade, the decline of labor unions, the shift in the work force from manu-

Figure 5. The percentage of full-time, year-round workers with low earnings has increased since 1979.

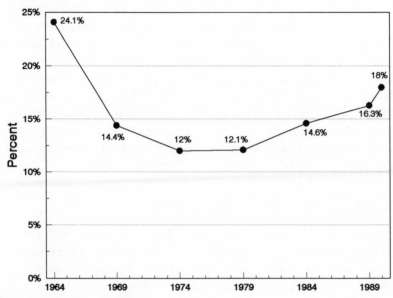

Source: U.S. Census Bureau

facturing to the service sector, and immigration. The relative importance of these factors varies greatly for different types of workers. It is difficult to single out the most important influence, because wage inequality has risen within each group of workers with similar educational, occupational, and industrial characteristics.[4] Even less clear are the reasons why these factors have contributed to earnings inequality.

Employer preference for more educated workers is no doubt an important contributor to the increasingly skewed earnings distribution, but its influence has been exaggerated. The fact that overall inequality has grown while educational attainment differentials have narrowed indicates that other factors are relevant. Moreover, the historical trends are not consistent. In the two decades following World War II, low earners experienced greater wage increases than high earners—a development little influenced by rising educational attainments.

Similarly, low earners in a wide variety of industries have lost ground in the past decade, which diminishes the importance that some have attached to industrial restructuring and international trade. Poor workers are less likely to benefit from union representation than other workers, but the decline of unions has probably significantly hurt the one-fifth of poor workers who labor in low-skilled blue-collar jobs. Less than one in six wage and salary workers now belong to unions, compared to roughly one in three at the peak point in the 1950s. The share of unionized operators, fabricators, and laborers has fallen from 39 to 26 percent since 1980. High unionization rates boost earnings in an occupation for both unionized and nonunionized workers, and, conversely, this steep drop has undoubtedly hurt both organized and unorganized poor workers in low-skilled blue-collar jobs.

The Demand for Low-Wage Workers

A healthy economy is the most obvious and the best single remedy for employment problems. During economic expansions, unemployment, involuntary part-time employment, discouraged workers, and the number of poor workers all tend to decline. Conversely, the labor-market hardships experienced by the working poor worsen during economic recessions because poor workers tend to be employed in the least stable jobs, and workers who lose better paying jobs compete with poor workers for the remaining employment opportunities. Economic growth alone, however, is only a partial solution of these problems. Overall economic growth does not reach all workers, including many poor workers who could benefit from education and training to qualify for better paying jobs.

The number and percentage of workers living in poverty fell sharply during the late 1960s, when the unemployment rate dipped below 4 percent and the minimum wage reached its peak inflation-adjusted value. Poverty among workers continued to fall in the early 1970s, when the unemployment rate ranged between 4.8 and 5.5 percent. Following a mid-decade recession, by 1979 a record low of only 2.1 percent of full-time, year-round workers were poor. Three years later the number of poor workers hit a post–World War II high as a consequence of back-to-back recessions and high inflation in the preceding years. By the late 1980s unemployment rates were at their lowest level since 1974, but the poverty rate for workers exceeded that in 1979. The subsequent 1990–91 recession again aggravated poverty among workers.

Uneven Growth

Economic growth by-passes large segments of the working poor because of employment barriers and persistently low wages. The barriers include the mismatch between their limited skills and the skills required in the available jobs. The working poor are also concentrated in industries whose prosperity is only loosely linked to general economic trends.

Poor workers may not benefit from overall economic growth if they are stranded in high-unemployment areas and cannot afford to move to areas where job opportunities exist. Rural poverty has often proved intractable even in the presence of nationwide economic expansion, Appalachia being the best-known example. In metropolitan areas, uneven development is also common. The suburban economy can flourish while the central city languishes, and pockets of poverty often exist side by side with booming development.[5] Many cities have recently experienced a renaissance that little benefits its poorer areas.

Uneven development has led to a debate whether a two-tier economy is polarizing American labor markets. This discussion is directly related to the fate of the working poor because if middle-income jobs decline, more workers are pushed into the low-wage job market and fewer will escape it. Some analysts argue that high-paying manufacturing jobs are declining while low-paying service jobs are on the rise.[6] They suggest, further, that technological change and international competition have exacerbated this situation.

Proponents of the two-tier or dual labor-market theory tend to overstate their case. The problems of low-wage workers are indeed growing, uneven development is a fact of the American economy, and American industry clearly no longer dominates the world economy, but it does not follow that middle-income jobs are declining sharply.

Technological Change

The claim that emerging new high-technology industries are eliminating middle-income jobs rests on two assumptions. The first is that these industries provide a high proportion of both high- and low-wage jobs, but few opportunities for middle-wage workers. The second assumption is that new technology displaces workers because computers replace administrative personnel and clerks, while robots replace low- or semi-skilled factory workers.

Persuasive evidence in support of these assumptions is lacking, however. Dislocation of workers by new technology has been an issue since the dawn of the industrial age. Echoing earlier assessments, a National Academy of Sciences review concluded that the adoption of new technology has probably played only a modest role in displacing jobs.[7] Technology renders some skills as well as jobs obsolete, but it is also the engine of progress that generates new jobs and raises productivity and living standards. Moreover, contrary to popular belief, new technology is typically introduced at a gradual pace.

The impact of technological change on job growth is complex. First, competitiveness may necessitate technological changes, so the real choice may be between losing some jobs now or losing many more jobs by not making the changes. Second, new technology that eliminates some tasks does not always cause a direct loss of jobs. Depending on the restructuring of the production process and company and public retraining policies, the new technology may create new tasks for the displaced workers. Third, the major reasons for the decline in the competitiveness of U.S. industries has been declining investment and reduced rate of productivity growth since the early 1970s. Thus there may be a need for greater investment in technology.

International Competition

International trade plays an unprecedented role in the U.S. and world economy. In 1991 U.S. merchandise imports and exports accounted for 15.7 percent of gross domestic product, more than double the proportion two decades earlier. The increased internationalization of the world economy has been a mixed blessing for the U.S. economy. Trade offers lower-priced goods to consumers, thus freeing some disposable income for purchasing other goods or services, but trade deficits have resulted in net employment losses due to cutbacks in domestic production. In addition, international trade dampens the growth of wages in the United States when firms cut costs to remain competitive. Workers often accept lower wages in fear of the alternative of no wages at all. Manufacturing employment, which peaked at 21.0 million in 1979, lost 2.6 million jobs during the next dozen years. Durable-goods industries paying above-average wages accounted for 2.2 million of the lost jobs, but it is unlikely that many of these displaced workers joined the ranks of the working poor. After reemployment formerly displaced workers earned on average almost as much as a typical worker. Even low-paid American workers cannot compete internationally on the basis of wages alone, particularly against Third World nations whose wages are a fraction of the U.S. minimum wage.

Migrant Farm Workers and Undocumented Immigrants

Because of their unique difficulties, the circumstances of migrant farm workers and undocumented immigrant workers deserve particular attention. Neither of these groups is adequately reflected in government statistics on poor workers. Due to their illegal status or transience, these workers either actively avoid survey enumerators or do not live at a fixed address, where they can be contacted by government enumerators.

Migrant and Seasonal Farm Workers

Many American farm workers and their families live and work under conditions that are cruel and harsh by any standard. The conclusions of the 1978 presidential commission that examined the problems of migrant and seasonal farm laborers remain valid today: "They are ill-housed, undernourished, face enormous health hazards, are underpaid, underemployed, undereducated, socially isolated, politically powerless, [and] excluded from much of the work-protective legislation that other American workers take for granted."[8]

Concern over the destitute plight of migrant and seasonal farm workers and their possible depression of wages among low earners led Congress to end the legalized large-scale importation of Mexican farm workers in 1964. The decline of cheap immigrant labor and widespread consumer sympathy demonstrated through boycotts enabled agricultural laborers to gain some improvement in working conditions.

The migrant and seasonal farm-worker population has decreased significantly due to the mechanization made possible by the growth of large-scale operations. Migrants, the poorest group, attained an estimated postwar high of 477,000 workers in 1959 before dropping by two-thirds during the next three decades. However, illegal aliens probably add several hundred thousand to the official count of migrant and seasonal farm workers.

Migrant and seasonal farm workers, together with domestic workers and day laborers, are most likely to be excluded from the legal and safety-net protections afforded other workers. Many states exempt migrant and seasonal farm workers from coverage under workers' compensation and unemployment insurance programs, and, even if they are covered, their meager earnings ensure that they receive little or no benefits. Although farm workers are legally eligible for other forms of assistance, the absence of records often makes it difficult for them to substantiate their low-income status and obtain benefits.[9]

Workplace protection laws are more likely to exclude than to cover migrant and seasonal farm workers. The federal minimum-wage law excluded farm workers until 1966, and it established a lower minimum for them until 1978. The current Fair Labor Standards Act's minimum-wage, child-labor and overtime provisions remain riddled with exceptions excluding farm workers. Even self-help opportunities are limited because farm laborers—unlike other workers—have no legal right to organize or join unions. In 1987, a full-time, year-round, minimum-wage job would have yielded 4 percent more than the average earnings of hired farm workers.

Federal social welfare programs have not completely neglected the pressing needs of migrant and seasonal farm workers. The largest programs provide education and training, at an estimated annual cost of $534 million:

	1992 appropriation (millions)	*Number assisted* (thousands)
Education		
Compensatory education	$308	343
Head Start	90	28
Employment and training		
Job Training Partnership Act	78	47
Employment service	NA	204
Migrant health program	58	500

Undocumented Immigrants

Federal law attempts to limit the number of immigrants but is often overwhelmed by foreigners seeking a better life and employers desiring cheap labor. Consequently, many undocumented aliens reside in the United States illegally. A large proportion of undocumented immigrants are poor, although they are often not counted in the published statistics. Many were poor upon entering the United States, they may lack schooling or facility in English, and their illegal status often bars them from taking advantage of assistance that could help them escape poverty.

To stem inflow of illegal immigrants, the 1986 Immigration Reform and Control Act instituted sanctions on employers who hired them. Employers face civil fines of up to $10,000 and a criminal penalty of up to $3,000 for each illegal alien hired, as well as a maximum six months' imprisonment. Ineffective enforcement, questionable voluntary compliance by employers, and reportedly widespread use of forged documents have frustrated efforts to reduce illegal immigration. Although admittedly a crude measure, border apprehensions are the only available gauge of illegal immigration. After dropping to 891,000 in 1989 following the amnesty law, apprehensions rose to 1,113,000 by 1991 despite a recession, which normally dampens the inflow.[10]

The 1986 immigration law also included a major humanitarian component by offering amnesty to immigrants who entered the country illegally. Three million illegal residents applied for amnesty under two separate provisions. Nearly 1.8 million applied under the program that granted amnesty to individuals who have lived in the United States continuously since 1982. Another 1.3

million applied for amnesty under a special provision for farm workers employed for at least ninety days between May 1985 and April 1986. As of February 1992, the U.S. Immigration and Naturalization Service (INS) had granted temporary residence status to 2.7 million applicants, 90 percent of the total. The INS estimated that roughly an additional 2 million to 3.5 million illegal immigrants resided in the United States in 1990.

Once granted temporary-residence status, the applicant had to demonstrate minimal knowledge of English and of U.S. history and government to qualify for permanent residence status. Congress appropriated $1 billion annually for four years beginning in 1988 to accommodate the increased social-program costs associated with newly legalized aliens. However, for five years amnestied individuals remained ineligible for federal welfare programs, except supplemental security income and Medicaid benefits and emergency services for pregnant women and children.

The vast majority of amnesty applicants were young single Mexican men. Over half of the total lived in California. Contrary to popular stereotypes, only a minority of those applying under the post-1981 residency provision were farm workers:

Prior to immigration	40%
First U.S. job	16
At time of application	8

These figures exclude the agricultural amnesty applicants because these individuals had an obvious incentive to claim that they were farm workers, and, given a flourishing market in forged documentation, their true occupational status is questionable. At the time of application, nearly two of every three aliens performed unskilled work as operators, fabricators, and laborers, or were employed in service jobs.

Amnesty applicants who reported their hourly wage earned 39 percent less than the median for all wage and salary workers in 1988: $5.00 versus $8.26 hourly (Figure 6). However, workers who had the longest tenure either in the United States or with one employer earned the highest wages among illegal immigrants, possibly indicating upward job mobility.

Refugees admitted to the United States under special provisions are another source of immigrants, numbering about 100,000 an-

Figure 6. Undocumented immigrants earned far less than total U.S. workers (1988).

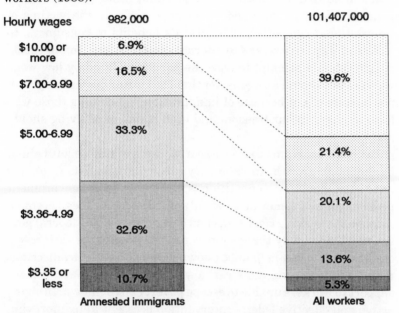

Sources: U.S. Immigration and Naturalization Service and U.S. Bureau of Labor Statistics

nually. In recent years they have originated primarily from Southeast Asia and the Soviet Union, and they are likely to be poor. Almost half reside in California. The law requires the federal government to reimburse states for some of the costs of providing refugees with cash and medical assistance during their first two years in the United States. In 1992 this assistance totaled $411 million.

Data are scarce on the effect of immigration, legal or illegal, on the wages of American citizens. Immigrant competition probably depresses the earnings of low-wage native workers, although to date researchers have not found strong or consistent effects.[11]

Whither the Low-Wage Job Market?

Much of the foregoing analysis demonstrates the need for more effective government policies to reduce the number of low-wage workers and improve their working conditions. A careful balance needs to be struck in both trade and immigration policies. Trade policies should be designed to consider not only the victims of international competition but also its benefits to consumers, to U.S. trading partners, and to international relations. Immigration policies should attempt to ease the hardships faced by low-wage workers but should also consider that the United States has grown not in spite of but because of immigration. Welcoming those who hope to share in our freedom and high standard of living should also be a goal.

Targeted programs to assist poor workers aid those left behind by economic growth. In secondary labor markets, where unions have little clout and competition is fierce, the federal government is the major and sometimes the only existing force able to promote reasonable working conditions and decent wages. The federal government can supply the resources needed to raise the skill levels of workers and can help knock down barriers created by discrimination. Federal programs can also provide income and service support to workers unable to escape poverty on their own. In short, active and effective federal intervention is essential to improving the difficult employment conditions of the working poor.

3

Federal Policies

4. Making Work Pay

The federal government directly influences working conditions through its minimum-wage and tax policies. The working poor and other low-wage workers often lack bargaining power and need a federal minimum to set a floor under their wages. The current floor is sagging, providing much weaker support than in the 1960s and 1970s. In 1992, full-time, year-round minimum-wage earnings provided an income equivalent to only an estimated 79 percent of the poverty line for a family of three.

In the first half of the 1980s, minimum-wage workers simultaneously faced a pay cut and an increasing federal tax burden. The 1986 tax-reform law reduced the tax burden, providing substantial relief to the working poor. The standard deduction, the personal exemption, and the earned income tax credit (EITC) rose, cutting or eliminating federal income taxes for millions of poor workers. Four years later the federal government further raised the EITC, although the credit continued to benefit only families with children.

The Federal Minimum Wage

The need for a federal minimum wage became apparent during the first few decades of this century. Both before and during the Great Depression, the free market did not provide minimally acceptable living standards for many workers, and the Supreme Court struck down state wage regulations. In 1937 the Court reversed its position, and a year later the federal Fair Labor

Standards Act established the first national wage standard. Since then, Congress has occasionally boosted the minimum wage and expanded its coverage to the vast majority of nonsupervisory employees. After a prolonged period of neglect, the 1989 minimum-wage amendments raised the hourly rate in two steps, from the previous rate of $3.35 to $4.25 an hour in April 1991, where it remained at the end of 1992.

The minimum-wage law directly and indirectly affects millions of workers. Detailed information on minimum-wage workers is only available for workers paid by the hour, and not for covered workers who are paid salaries. About four of five minimum-wage workers are paid hourly rates. Following the 1991 minimum-wage increase, 5.7 million hourly workers earned the minimum wage or less. Another 8.5 million workers received wages just above this level; many of these workers also received raises when the federal standard increased.

	Total	*Below minimum*	*At minimum*	*$4.26–5.00*
Workers (millions)	61.8	2.4	3.4	8.5

Earnings of workers paid by the hour, 1991

Part-time employees and women each account for almost two-thirds of minimum-wage workers. Although blacks and Hispanics account for a disproportionately large share of minimum-wage workers, non-Hispanic whites constitute seven in ten minimum-wage workers. Contrary to a common misconception, only 29 percent of minimum-wage workers are teenagers. Another 22 percent are aged 20 to 24, and half are aged 25 or older. Millions of minimum-wage workers significantly boost their families' living standards.

More than half of minimum-wage workers are employed in retail trade; another quarter work in services. Both industries employ a large share of poor workers. Minimum-wage employees are also overrepresented among occupations such as private-household workers and farm laborers. Some employers or occupations are not covered by minimum-wage protections.

Most poor workers have earnings that cluster around the minimum wage. The Congressional Budget Office estimated that one

Figure 7. The inflation-adjusted value of the minimum wage is well below its value in the 1960s and the 1970s (current and 1992 dollars).

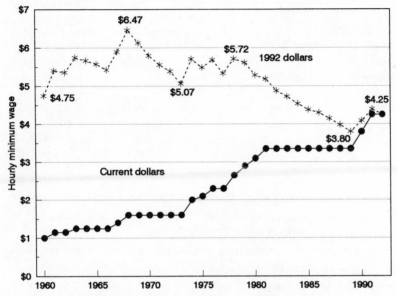

Sources: U.S. Labor Department and U.S. Census Bureau

in four impoverished workers paid hourly rates in March 1987 earned the minimum wage (then equal to $3.35 an hour) or less. Another one in three of these workers earned between $3.36 and $4.35 an hour. Altogether, 57 percent of poor workers had hourly earnings of $4.35 an hour or less. However, a study of poor minimum-wage workers that combined both those paid by the hour and those not paid by the hour found that an even larger share of poor workers earn the minimum wage; it found that 4.1 million (half of poor workers) earned the minimum wage or less in 1988. Forty percent of these workers were adult men.[1] A large majority of minimum-wage workers escape poverty, mostly because of other household members' income. The appropriate level of the minimum wage should be judged in light of its effects on workers from both poor and nonpoor families.

A Sagging Floor

The minimum wage remained at $3.35 an hour from January 1981 through March 1990, despite a 48 percent rise in the cost of

Table 5. The value of the minimum wage since the 1960s

Period	1992 dollars	Percentage of poverty line, family of three	Percentage of average nonsupervisory wage
1960s	$5.65	104.7%	52.2%
1970s	5.54	102.6	45.8
1980s	4.52	83.9	40.4
1992	4.25	78.8	39.8

Source: U.S. Bureau of Labor Statistics

living during this period. The April 1990 and 1991 increases in the minimum wage made up less than half of the ground lost to inflation during the 1980s.

As a result, the minimum wage remains far below its peak levels of support in the 1960s and 1970s (Figure 7). If the minimum wage had the same purchasing power in 1992 that it had on average in the 1970s, it would equal $5.54 an hour instead of $4.25 an hour. In 1992 the minimum wage equaled only about 40 percent of the average wage for production or nonsupervisory workers. During the 1950s and the 1960s Congress generally set the minimum wage at about 50 percent of the average wage in private industry. In the 1970s the minimum wage averaged 46 percent of the average wage. It also bears noting that the expansions in the earned income tax credit in 1986 and 1990 fell short of compensating for the decline of the value of the minimum wage.

Only a worker living alone on minimum-wage earnings escapes poverty. A full-time, year-round minimum-wage worker earned $8,840 in 1992, which was $2,400 less than the estimated 1992 poverty threshold of $11,210 for a family of three, and $5,500 less than the poverty threshold of $14,380 for a family of four. (The average working poor family has 3.8 members.) In contrast, throughout most of the 1960s and the 1970s, full-time minimum-wage earnings were sufficient to bring a family of three out of poverty (Table 5 and Figure 8).

As the federal minimum wage declined, some states raised their minimums above the national standard. In April 1992 seven states

Figure 8. Since 1980, minimum-wage earnings for a full-time, year-round worker have fallen below the poverty line for a three-member family.

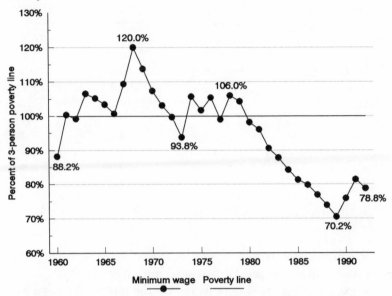

Sources: U.S. Labor Department and U.S. Census Bureau

and the District of Columbia had minimum wages higher than the federal minimum. These state standards, however, affect only the 8 percent of the labor force that resides in these jurisdictions. Moreover, the minimum wage in these states is still below the peak historic levels of the federal minimum. Federal action is required for the minimum wage to provide more substantial support.

The Unprotected

As the figure of 2.4 million workers paid by the hour who earned less than the minimum wage in 1991 testifies, the minimum wage does not protect all workers. In 1990 exemptions applied to 10.8 million private nonsupervisory employees (Table 6), and 2.9 million outside sales workers were unprotected. Teenagers are covered by the law but may receive a subminimum wage. Many employees are denied minimum-wage earnings because employers violate the law. Poor workers are presumably highly repre-

Table 6. Variation in the percentage of the work force denied minimum-wage protection by industry (1990 in millions)

Industry	Total	Covered	Exempt
Total private	81.7	70.9	10.8
Agriculture	1.7	0.7	1.1
Manufacturing	16.9	16.4	0.5
Wholesale trade	5.5	4.4	1.1
Retail trade	17.9	16.2	1.7
Finance, insurance, and real estate	5.9	4.4	1.4
Service industries	21.7	17.2	4.5
Private household	1.3	0.9	0.4
Other	10.8	10.7	0.1

Source: U.S. Bureau of Labor Statistics

sented among those uncovered or illegally paid less than the minimum wage, although precise numbers are unavailable.

The proportion of workers covered by the minimum wage has increased considerably since the law's establishment. The 1938 Fair Labor Standards Act covered only one in four workers, but by 1990 the law covered 87 percent of all private nonsupervisory employees. All nonsupervisory employees employed by government—11.2 million workers—are also covered by the minimum wage.

In fiscal 1989 the U.S. Labor Department identified $29 million in back wages due because of minimum-wage violations. Employers agreed to pay $21 million of the wages owed to 124,000 employees. The department inspects only 2 to 3 percent of all establishments subject to the Fair Labor Standards Act each year, mostly in response to employee complaints. Usually an employer found in violation of this act is obliged to pay only the differential between the actual amount paid and the amount that should have been paid under the minimum wage. This practice enables employers to break the law with impunity.

More than a decade ago, the Minimum Wage Study Commission estimated that in 1979 only about one-fifth of the estimated dollar amount of FLSA violations were detected.[2] Over 70 percent of total minimum-wage violations occur under the provision that allows employers to deduct costs of certain food, lodging, and other expenses customarily provided to minimum-wage workers. These violations can sometimes be due to technical mistakes in calculating wages, as opposed to willful violations of the law. The percentage of violations currently detected is almost certainly lower than in 1979. Despite the growth in the work force during the past decade, both the amount of staff time spent on enforcement—558 staff years in 1981 and 402 a decade later—as well as the real level of fines have fallen.

Some minimum-wage violations should be the cause for special concern. In 1982 the Labor Standards Subcommittee of the U.S. Congress House Education and Labor Committee found widespread evidence of sweatshops in the needle trades. The subcommittee chairman described an employee-employer relationship in which "an undereducated, underskilled, usually illegal worker is compelled by economic desperation to work under intolerable, less than subsistence conditions, abused and unprotected from the most fundamental forms of industrial exploitation."[3] In 1988, based on interviews with federal and state officials, the U.S. General Accounting Office found that sweatshops were widespread, especially in the restaurant, apparel, manufacturing, and meat-processing industries. Three of every four officials surveyed "said sweatshops were a serious problem in at least one industry in their geographical area."[4]

The exact extent of sweatshops and the size of their employment force are unknown. Presumably many of these workers are poor, but many may not be reflected in official statistics because they are not legal U.S. residents. Undocumented workers rarely report illegal or inadequate workplace conditions because they are unaware of labor laws, are afraid of losing their jobs, or fear deportation. In addition to the effect on workers, law-abiding employers are placed at a disadvantaged when other employers illegally pay less than the minimum wage.

A Help or a Hindrance?

Policymakers and economists have long debated whether the income benefits of a higher minimum wage outweigh the negative effects of lost employment. Proponents argue that the minimum wage increases living standards and promotes the work ethic. Opponents contend that the minimum wage hurts low-wage employees because it reduces demand for workers and therefore results in fewer jobs.

The minimum wage is a statement by society that compensation below a certain amount is unacceptable. Most employees are protected from substandard work conditions by their special skills, benign employer practices, or unions. But low-wage workers often do not enjoy these advantages, and federal intervention is necessary to ensure socially acceptable employment standards.

Many individuals and families benefit from the mandated minimum. The wage floor helps some escape poverty and lessens its severity for others. For minimum-wage earners who are not poor, the extra income is often essential. A teenager can save more money to pay for school costs, or a family may scrape together enough money to afford more than the bare necessities.

Studies of the minimum wage tend to focus on employment effects and to ignore its equally important income effects. The limited evidence that is available does indicate, however, that the income effects have been positive. In 1981, when the hourly minimum wage was raised from $3.10 to $3.35, the Department of Labor estimated that the potential aggregate increase amounted to $2.2 billion annually, and that 5.5 million workers were eligible to receive raises. The income effects of prior raises were of equivalent size. Similar estimates for the 1990 and 1991 minimum-wage increases are not available.

The minimum wage also encourages individuals to work rather than to depend on welfare. When individuals earn their keep instead of relying on government support, they not only gain the satisfaction of helping themselves but also enhance their opportunities for upward mobility. Society benefits from increased output and reduced public-assistance costs. An inadequate statutory minimum wage discourages the poor from seeking employment. When the working poor toil for little more—and sometimes less—than government cash and noncash benefits, work can be seen as a less desirable or futile alternative.

Job Loss

Statutory increases in the minimum wage do result in some job loss. However, minimum-wage opponents tend to overstate both the extent of job loss and the applicability of market theory to the functioning of low-wage labor markets. Economists have attempted to measure employment losses due to the statutory minimum, but the complexity of the economic factors involved renders the results speculative. Nevertheless, a few general conclusions are warranted.

The minimum wage has its largest disemployment effect on young workers because they are less likely to be hired and more likely to be laid off than adults, and because a smaller proportion of adults works at the minimum. Basing their findings on labor market data through 1979, economists for the congressionally mandated Minimum Wage Study Commission estimated that a 10 percent increase in the minimum wage decreased teenage employment by about 1 percent.[5] Today's low-wage labor markets, however, differ from the labor markets of the 1960s and 1970s, and the value of the minimum wage is considerably less. The commission's estimates, therefore, are not directly applicable to the 1990s. A more recent study replicated the commission's methodology using data through 1986. The study found that the corresponding teenage job loss was 0.6 percent for a 10 percent minimum-wage increase, and that adult workers would sustain no loss.[6]

Studies focusing on the most recent round of minimum-wage increases are even more telling. Two recent studies of the effects of the federal minimum-wage increases in 1990 and 1991 found that the increases did not result in employment losses.[7] A third study, which analyzed the impact when California raised its minimum wage above the federal standard, yielded similar results.[8]

These recent studies underscore how the employment effect of a change in the minimum wage varies with economic conditions and demographic trends. The lower real value of the minimum wage and the decline of teenage-labor-force participation in the 1980s, in contrast to teenage-labor-force growth in the 1960s and the 1970s, may have reduced the employment effects of moderate increases in the minimum wage.

Estimates of job losses caused by the minimum wage should be viewed as ballpark guesses. Objections to a statutory floor under wages are grounded more in free-market theory than in empirical evidence. According to that theory, if government sets the minimum wage above the wage workers would otherwise receive, the demand for workers drops and the supply of workers rises because higher earnings induce more workers to seek jobs. The inevitable result, according to the theory, is that fewer workers are employed and that the unemployment rate rises.

In practice this theory does not fully describe the actions of employers and employees. Higher wages may enhance job stability and attachment to the work force. In turn, employers may respond by reorganizing the production process to make better use of existing employees. As a result of increased productivity, the actual cost of labor may not increase as much as the rise in the minimum wage. Also, because minimum-wage firms compete with one another, raising the minimum wage for all firms, as long as coverage is complete and enforcement is effective, will not give one firm a competitive advantage over another.

Some firms may set their pay scales at the minimum wage, even if the minimum wage is below the market clearing price. In these cases, raising the minimum wage would actually increase employment as workers who refuse openings at lower wages might accept jobs at a higher pay. Under such circumstances, absent a mandated minimum-wage increase, firms may eventually have to adjust their wages upward, but market reactions are not as quick and smooth as predicted by free market theory. Minimum-wage employers are reluctant to raise their pay scales unless there is a federally mandated increase in the minimum.

The minimum wage has scant impact on other general economic conditions. Because the vast majority of workers earn considerably more than the minimum wage, it has only a minuscule effect on the inflation rate. In any event, workers who earn the minimum wage should not shoulder a disproportionate financial burden in the fight against inflation.

Youth Subminimum Wage

Since 1961 employers have been able to pay full-time students 85 percent of the minimum wage if the student works fewer than twenty hours a week. In fiscal 1989, an estimated 89,000 students were certified for employment under this program. The Reagan and Bush administrations have argued that a broader subminimum wage would reduce the high level of teenage unemployment and that work experience is more important for youngsters than earnings.

As part of a compromise necessary to secure the most recent increase in the minimum wage, in 1989 the federal government expanded the scope of the teenage subminimum wage. Under the new so-called training wage, a subminimum wage equal to 85 percent of the minimum wage applies to a teenager's first ninety days on a job, whether or not on-the-job training is provided. Teenagers may be paid the subminimum wage for a second ninety-day period only if they work for a different employer and this new employer has an on-the-job training program that meets criteria established by the U.S. Labor Department. The subminimum training wage provision is currently scheduled to expire in March 1993.

Proponents of the new subminimum contend it encourages employers to hire young, inexperienced workers. They argue that employers should be able to pay these teenagers the subminimum wage until their productivity rises to a level that would justify the regular minimum wage. Early evidence indicates that the subminimum training wage has had little effect because it has not been used. A survey of fast-food restaurants in Texas found that less than one in twenty used the new youth subminimum.[9] In addition, as of May 1992, two years after enactment of the subminimum provision, only fourteen employers nationwide had requested Labor Department approval for the *second* ninety-day subminimum training wage.

The value of a blanket youth subminimum appears to be dubious. Many youths, including those who need the most help, would suffer an income loss. It is unlikely to induce substantial hiring of disadvantaged youths. Youths from poor families who have trouble breaking into the labor force often lack skills and connections to the job market. They need to master the Three R's and require specialized programs, such as those offered by the Job Corps, to prepare them for the job market. Job creation prospects should be viewed with further skepticism because youths have alternative uses for their time. In some labor markets, there is evidence that the minimum pay youth would accept (what economists call a reservation wage) is higher than the regular minimum wage, let alone a subminimum. In addition, a youth subminimum may harm poor adult workers who labor at the minimum wage, to the extent that employers substitute teenagers for older workers. Lastly, employers hiring economically disadvantaged youths are already eligible for up to a 40 percent wage subsidy under the Targeted Jobs Tax Credit (discussed in chapter 6).

A Prudent Policy

Restoring the minimum wage to its traditional level of support—50 percent of the average private nonsupervisory hourly wage—would have required an increase of $1.10 to $5.35 (1992 dollars). This would enable full-time minimum-wage earners to reach the poverty line for a family of three. The raise should occur by steps, in order to smooth necessary adjustments. The wage should then be indexed to inflation or average wage growth to prevent future erosion. At whatever level the minimum wage is set, the protection it offers is sharply diminished if the law is not enforced. Congress should enact legislation to improve enforcement and raise the fines for violators.

Strengthening the minimum-wage standard would not lift all of the working poor out of poverty. A sizable proportion of poor workers are self-employed or otherwise uncovered by the minimum-wage law, and many part-year or part-time minimum-wage workers would still have annual earnings below the poverty line. Nevertheless, some families would be raised above the poverty threshold by a higher minimum wage, and the others might be lifted out of poverty by the earned income tax credit or food stamps. Those who remain poor would face less severe income problems. Although most minimum-wage workers are not poor, the nonpoor also would benefit from a raise.

A prudent minimum-wage policy should balance the prevention of job losses with the benefits of eliminating unacceptably low pay. If the minimum wage is set too high, the working poor and other minimum-wage workers may indeed suffer more than they gain. More than half a century of federal experience with the minimum wage suggests that if the floor under wages is set at one-half of the average hourly pay of nonsupervisory workers, the resulting disemployment effects remain relatively insignificant, but the accompanying income boosts are instrumental in alleviating deprivation and in encouraging economic self-sufficiency.

Taxation

Although government statistics define poverty by pre-tax income, in real life after-tax income determines disposable income and purchasing power. The three largest components of the federal tax system are the personal income tax, the social security tax, and the corporate income tax. The 1986 tax reform law relieved most low-income workers from paying the personal income tax. However, the social security payroll tax continues to be a considerable burden on poor workers. In 1992 workers paid 7.65 percent on every dollar earned annually up to $55,500, matched by an identical tax paid by employers. The corporate income tax affects the poor only indirectly, to the extent that it is passed on to consumers in the form of higher prices, but economists generally believe that the wealthy bear a greater burden of this tax. Other, lesser features of the federal tax code—such as excise taxes—tend to be regressive.

In addition to the tax rate, three aspects of the federal personal income tax system significantly affect the poor. First, the standard deduction—the amount of income exempt from taxation—is available to all taxpayers who do not itemize their deductions, which few poor workers do. Second, each taxpayer and dependent is entitled to a personal exemption, whose full value is subtracted from a household's taxable income. Third, the EITC, which was enacted in 1975 to offset rising social security payroll taxes and to promote work, benefits specifically low-income families with children. If the credit exceeds a parent's tax bill, the difference is refundable to the taxpayer.

The 1986 Tax Reform Act

Federal taxes paid by low-wage workers rose in the first half of the 1980s as social security taxes increased and provisions in the federal income tax system benefiting low- and middle-income workers failed to keep pace with inflation, thus increasing the effective tax rate. In 1979 a family of four did not pay federal income taxes until its income exceeded the poverty line by 16 percent; in 1986 the income tax threshold for this family was 14 percent *below* the poverty line. Combining the personal income tax with the social security payroll tax, the effective federal tax rate for a family of four at the poverty line rose from 4.0 percent in 1978 to 10.4 percent in 1986.

The 1986 tax bill reduced or eliminated some tax credits or deductions, but also lowered marginal income tax rates. The law benefited poor workers by raising the standard deduction, the personal exemption, and the EITC. As a result, the federal tax burden on the poor fell to the levels of the late 1970s. By 1988, when the 1986 changes were fully in effect and adjusted for inflation, a family of four did not owe income tax until its income was 25 percent above the poverty line. If the family had a poverty-level income, it faced a combined income and payroll tax rate of 2.1 percent. From 1978 to 1988, the combined income and payroll tax rate of a four-member family at the poverty line changed as follows:

1978	4.0%
1982	9.6
1986	10.4
1988	2.1

Depending on the type of household, the 1986 law increased the standard deduction by $500 to $1,900. The law nearly doubled the value of each personal exemption, from $1,080 in 1986 to $2,000 in 1989. Finally, the EITC specifically targeted the needs of working poor families with children. Congress raised the maximum size of the credit by nearly a half and indexed it to inflation for the first time.

Earned Income Tax Credit

The federal EITC has become one of the most important government benefits to poor workers, receiving widespread support from liberals and conservatives alike.[10] In 1992, 13 million families received an average credit of $800, at a cost of $10.7 billion to the federal treasury. The refundable aspect of the credit is crucial; without it the family that owes no taxes would not benefit from

Figure 9. The value of the EITC for a family with one child started to phase out when earnings rose above $11,480 in 1992.

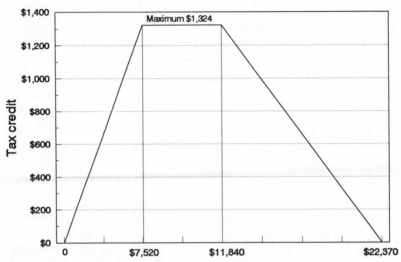

Source: U.S. Congress, Joint Committee on Taxation

the credit because virtually all working-poor families are exempt from income taxes.

The credit is strongly pro-work because nonworking parents do not qualify. Moreover, while welfare benefits fall sharply as earnings rise, the EITC rises with earnings for the very poor. The same credit is available to two-parent and single-parent families. The credit is also pro-family because it is extended only to custodial parents—those who live with their children more than half the year.

The 1986 EITC expansion more than recaptured the ground that the credit lost to inflation in the first half of the 1980s. Amendments in 1990, when fully implemented, will increase the size of the basic EITC by another 70 percent by 1994. In 1992 the basic EITC provided a 17.6 percent credit for each dollar earned up to $7,520. At that level of earnings, a family with one child qualified for the maximum credit of $1,324. The credit remained at $1,324 until a family's earnings or adjusted gross income surpassed $11,840. The benefit is then phased out, declining 13.2 cents for each dollar earned until the credit falls to zero at an income of $22,370 (Figure 9). In addition, the 1990 legislation established a slightly larger credit for families with two or more children. By 1994, the maximum credit will be 23 percent of earnings for families with one child, and 25 percent for families with two or more children. As a result of the enlarged EITC, the net effect of income and payroll taxes will be to boost the income of the average family of four at the poverty line.

The 1990 law also added supplemental credits for families with children under 1 year old and for families incurring health-insurance premiums for a policy that covers a child. In addition, the legislation stipulated that EITC payments would not reduce benefits from other programs—Aid to Families with Dependent Children, Supplemental Security Income, food stamps, Medicaid, and subsidized housing. In part, the 1990 EITC expansion was designed to offset other tax provisions of the 1990 deficit reduction package that were regressive, taking a larger share of income from the poor than from the middle class or the wealthy.

Despite the recent substantial improvements in the EITC, subject to budget constraints, further reforms might be considered. The first would be to provide larger EITC benefits for bigger families. Family needs, of course, increase with family size. Welfare benefits also rise with family size, but wages do not, and consequently low-wage work becomes less competitive with welfare as family size grows. Under current law the maximum difference in EITC benefit levels by family size is limited to $160 a year by 1994. The law also provides no additional credit for families with more than two children, although 60 percent of all children in working-poor families live in such families. Moreover, the poverty rate among working families with three or more children is more than twice the poverty rate of working families with one or two children. Finally, an expansion of the EITC to poor workers without children might also be considered.

A second problem with the EITC is that more than 99 percent of its beneficiaries receive their benefits in the form of a tax refund after the end of the tax year. Since 1979, federal law has permitted workers to receive the EITC in their regular paychecks, but many employers and low-income working families are unaware of this option.[11] While some recipients prefer receiving the EITC in one lump-sum payment, the credit would likely be more effective in meeting ongoing household needs and as a work incentive if it were provided as part of the regular paycheck throughout the year. Similarly, the EITC is likely to be more attractive than welfare if received in the regular paycheck, because a family may compare its potential take-home pay to its monthly AFDC check.

For the EITC to be fully effective, strengthened outreach efforts are also necessary to ensure that eligible families receive the credit. Because federal income tax liabilities have been eliminated for most working poor families with children, many families may conclude there is no reason to file a tax return. If they do not file, they cannot receive a refundable credit. Some EITC outreach efforts have been launched by public officials, as well as business, labor, religious, charitable, and other nonprofit organizations. The Internal Revenue Service has also stepped up efforts to inform low-wage workers about the EITC.

Other Tax Reforms

Recent tax reforms have greatly benefited working poor families with children. Because tax deductions reduce the income subject to taxation, additional tax deductions will not benefit most poor workers since they do not owe any income taxes to begin with. Poor workers and their families can be helped, however, through increased *refundable* tax credits. For example, converting the current deduction for the personal exemption into a refundable credit for all children would be of much benefit to working-poor families, but at a high cost to the federal treasury.

The working poor who live alone or who live in families without children have been less well-served by recent tax code changes. They did benefit from the increases in the standard deduction and the personal exemption but were denied the EITC. In fact, because federal taxes other than the income tax were raised significantly in the 1980s, poor workers who are childless couples or who live alone often faced an increased tax burden. For example, the total federal effective tax rate on the poorest fifth of nonelderly families without children rose from 10.9 percent in 1980 to a projected 15.0 percent in 1993.[12] In 1992 a childless working couple with poverty-level earnings of $9,467 owed $724 in social security payroll taxes. Further attention should be paid to relieving the tax burden on all of the working poor, and not just families with children.

Finally, less progress has been made at the state and local

levels in designing taxes that do not burden the working poor excessively. States and localities are heavily dependent on regressive state and local sales and property taxes. State income taxes are also typically less progressive than federal income taxes, although six states have recently enacted their own earned income tax credit.

Combining EITC with Minimum Wages

The merits of the EITC have led some to view the policy as a substitute for the minimum wage, but the two programs are best viewed as complementary policies. In 1992 the disposable (after-tax) income of full-time, year-round minimum-wage workers was $1,700 below the estimated poverty line for a family of three, and $4,900 short of the estimated poverty line for a family of four.

To close these gaps, some analysts have proposed further EITC expansions. This option would not discourage hiring because the direct cost of labor to employers would not change—although federal treasury revenue would decline—and it would be better targeted than the minimum wage to poor workers. However, the minimum wage needs to be raised as well, for several reasons. First, nonpoor low-wage workers would benefit more from a raise in the minimum wage, and recent income trends suggest that moderate- and middle-income families could also use a boost. Second, given the federal deficit, the large cost of relying too heavily on a further EITC expansion to help the working poor is likely to impede passage. Without a larger minimum wage, expanding the EITC enough to close the poverty gap for all full-time, year-round workers would carry a price tag of billions of dollars. Raising the minimum wage, a private-sector approach, also would provide the poor with more *earned* income, which is preferable to a government income transfer. Finally, the EITC is almost always received in one lump-sum payment; most poor workers are better served if the income is delivered in each paycheck, as occurs with the minimum wage.

A two-pronged policy approach is appropriate, with the private sector bearing the costs of the minimum wage, and the public sector bearing the costs of the EITC. The minimum wage should be restored to its traditional level of support, when full-time minimum-wage earnings would lift a family of three out of poverty. An EITC with a larger adjustment for family size could then help families of four or more to escape poverty.

Establishing labor conditions that help lift workers out of poverty on their own accord is the best mechanism to improve the lot of the working poor. It is preferable for workers to earn their way out of poverty than for government to provide additional income support or in-kind benefits. The right mix of low federal taxes, refundable tax credits, and an adequate federal minimum wage will permit more workers to escape poverty on their own.

5. *Removing Employment Obstacles*

The poor confront many obstacles in obtaining jobs that pay a wage adequate to achieve self-sufficiency. The level of educational attainment has risen in the United States, but many individuals still lack basic skills. These individuals have great difficulty competing in today's labor market, and their difficulties are often transferred to the next generation. The children of the poor and unskilled are more likely than children from affluent families to be inadequately prepared when they enter the work force.

The quality of education largely determines the skill levels of American workers. Some individuals fall through the cracks and require a second chance to acquire the basic skills necessary for sustained employment. Federal programs have opened opportunities to unskilled or disabled adults, and the need for such assistance continues to rise. The provision of basic skills acts as preventive medicine, by enhancing the earnings of unskilled workers.

Many poor individuals with adequate job skills face other obstacles in finding or holding better paid jobs. Employment discrimination remains a barrier, preventing some minorities and women from obtaining sustained full-time work. For poor parents, the lack of adequate, affordable childcare can be an insurmountable obstacle. Federal policies have addressed these problems through the enforcement of equal employment opportunity laws and the provision of social services.

Low Skills and Low Earnings

Inadequate education or work-related skills are powerful causes of poverty. Conversely, growing up poor significantly reduces the likelihood that children will obtain a proper education. To alleviate the dire consequences of this potentially vicious circle, remedial policies should include education and training, as well as broader antipoverty measures.

The educational attainment of poor workers has increased in recent decades: almost two-thirds now complete high school, compared with an identical proportion who never obtained a diploma two decades ago. Yet in 1990 one of six workers aged 20 or older without a high school education was poor, compared with one in fifty college graduates.[1]

Education	Poor workers (distribution)	Poverty rate 1990	Poverty rate 1979
Total	7,373,000	6.1%	5.3%
High school dropout	36.2%	15.7	11.1
High school only	41.9	6.3	4.5
Some college	14.3	4.1	3.8
College graduate	7.7	1.9	2.2

More poignantly, while the overall poverty rate among workers grew somewhat during the past decade, it rose significantly among the least educated. The earned income of adults aged 25 to 64 provides further evidence regarding the impact of educational attainment (Figure 10).

The labor-market disadvantages of the deficiently educated by no means imply that poverty among workers could be eliminated by ensuring that all youngsters completed high school. The educational process not only provides skills but also sorts individuals by ability or credentials. Poverty, earnings, and productivity trends do not correlate closely with the extraordinary rise in high school graduates among the work force in recent decades. The fact that overall income inequality has grown while educational attainment differentials have narrowed also indicates that factors other than education have significantly influenced wage trends.

Nonetheless, it is indisputable that a lack of basic skills usually limits earning potential or impedes individuals from even secur-

Figure 10. Three-fifths of individuals aged 25 to 64 with less than a high school education earned less than $10,000 or did not work at all (1990).

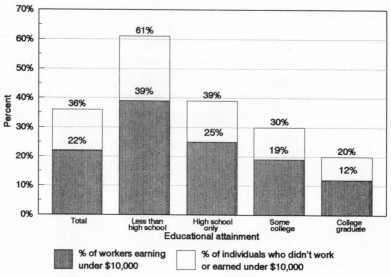

Source: U.S. Census Bureau

ing work. Although difficult to define, illiteracy is the most serious deficiency. Basic competency is essential for even most entry-level jobs. In 1982 (the latest available data, but in all likelihood conditions have not significantly improved since then), 19 million Americans (13 percent) aged 20 or older were judged functionally illiterate, including 29 percent of those with incomes less than $10,000 in 1981. To pass this literacy test, individuals had to correctly answer twenty out of twenty-six questions. Virtually all questions related to forms that might be encountered at a social security, welfare, or doctor's office. Some of the questions involved choosing "the answer that means the same as the word or phrase with an underline under it." The first question was:

Persons may receive benefits if they are eligible.
    a. qualified
    b. complete
    c. single
    d. logical

Illiteracy was strongly correlated with the educational attainment of individuals aged 20 to 39.

Education	*Illiteracy rate*
Less than high school	27%
High school only	6
College	1

The working poor with no more than a high school education are roughly equally divided between dropouts and graduates. Dropout rates continue to decline, but remain disturbingly high.

	Estimated 1990 dropout rate
Total	23%
Hispanic	35
Black	30
White	19

Many dropouts—perhaps as many as half—reenroll later, most of them in high school equivalency programs. However, the brevity of many programs, and the probability that bearers of equivalency degrees will earn less than high school graduates, reinforces the importance of attaining a high school diploma.[2]

Individuals with no more than a high school education are often locked out of the better paid jobs that permit escape from poverty. During the past two decades, the inflation-adjusted income of individuals with less than a high education has fallen, and the income of those with diplomas or equivalency degrees has barely kept pace with inflation.[3]

Second-Chance Programs

The deficient skills of poor workers stem from an inadequate education, but it is difficult to predict who will later become impoverished workers. In contrast to the formal education system, largely funded by state and local governments, most "second-chance" education and training for those who failed or were failed by traditional schooling is subsidized by the federal government. Total public education expenditures dwarf the federal investment in training. This distribution is appropriate because learning rates are highest during childhood, and adult assistance often has but a marginal impact in boosting credentials and earnings. Thus efforts to enhance the future skills of those who may experience poverty as adults must concentrate on children, but should not ignore the needs of currently poor adults.

Most second-chance education and training initiatives began as part of the 1960s antipoverty policies. Because of their recent origins, the programs have undergone considerable transformation in an evolution by no means completed. Public policy in the past five years has increasingly emphasized education, with substantially more funding for adult education and welfare recipients (discussed in chapter 7).

Adult Education

Adult education programs, funded largely by state and local governments, have grown significantly in the past decade, although assistance remains well below national needs. In 1992 spending by all levels of government probably exceeded $1 billion, more than triple that in 1980 (adjusted for inflation), and enrollment increased by 75 percent to 3.6 million students by 1990. Federal adult education outlays dropped during the Reagan years but have since risen significantly.

In 1990 two-fifths of adult education participants worked, and an equal proportion looked for work. Given the fact that 70 percent enrolled at the elementary school level, undoubtedly the majority were poor. The proportion of students who enrolled in English-as-a-second-language classes has grown from a fifth to a third since 1980, spurred by the 1986 immigration law, which enabled millions of illegal aliens to legally remain in the United States contingent upon a minimum knowledge of English. The federal government also committed $4 billion for the 1988–1993 period to compensate states for various social services provided to the newly legalized immigrants. Education is one of the three major components of this fund, but no information has yet been collected on how the states have spent it.

Due to limited federal monitoring, little is known about the effectiveness of adult education programs or how to improve them. Adult education program expenditures per participant averaged only $236 (1992 dollars) in 1989, but it is impossible to judge the significance of this amount because adult education is supplemented substantially by local schools and social programs. The 1991 National Literacy Act required states to implement indicators to assess program quality.

Despite important improvements in the past decade, those who most need adult education are least likely to obtain it. In 1990 one-fifth of working individuals in households with an annual income of less than $10,000 were enrolled in some form of adult education—but this was half the 41 percent rate for all workers.[4] Poor workers also obtain little financial assistance to pursue postsecondary education. One of ten working-poor families benefited from federal postsecondary education assistance, while 5 percent received state, local, or private postsecondary aid. Nonpoor workers were more likely to receive adult education through the private sector. Many who could benefit from adult education fail to enroll due to embarrassment or negative attitudes toward school.

Job Training

Federal job training programs for the unemployed began with $10 million appropriated as part of the 1961 Area Redevelopment Act and rose more than a thousandfold within two decades before declining sharply. The second step was the 1962 Manpower Development and Training Act, originally targeted at workers displaced by automation, but quickly redirected toward the impoverished. President Johnson's antipoverty initiatives experimented with a wide variety of training programs, most of which Congress consolidated under the Comprehensive Employment and Training Act (CETA) in 1973, which was in turn replaced in 1982 by the current Job Training Partnership Act (JTPA). In 1981 the federal government cut employment and training funding severely, and current expenditures are now less than a third of the peak level in the late 1970s. Between fiscal 1989 and 1992, total JTPA funding was stable (adjusted for inflation), with some components gaining and others losing.

The federal government funds more than a dozen employment and training programs. JTPA itself contains six separate components, including the Job Corps, assistance for dislocated workers, and subsidized jobs for teenagers during summer vacation. Most programs concentrate on assistance for employable, low-income individuals. About three-fourths of adult JTPA participants were

Figure 11. Federal support of employment and training programs has declined sharply since the 1970s (1992 dollars).

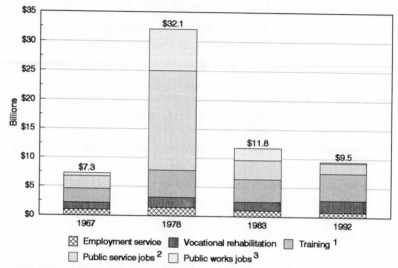

1. Classroom or on-the-job training and work-welfare programs
2. CETA employment and work experience jobs and other programs discussed in chapter 6
3. Construction or rehabilitation

Sources: U.S. Office of Management and Budget, *Budget of the U.S. Government,* various years; U.S. Congressional Research Service

either working or looking for work in the year before enrolling. The programs serve youth and young adults in greater numbers than their proportion in the eligible population. Employment and training programs provide a wide variety of services, although few enrollees receive more than one form of assistance.

JTPA's largest component (Title IIA) funds training or job-search assistance to more than a million individuals annually, as follows:

Classroom training	40%
Job-search assistance and minor services	35
On-the-job training	18
Work experience	7

Nearly half of enrollees are younger than 22 years old. Adjusted for inflation, between 1989 and 1992 the federal government cut

Title IIA appropriations by 13 percent. Most classroom and on-the-job training is for low-skilled jobs. Half of all occupationally specific training was for the following positions: clerk/typist, secretary, or word processor; electronic assembler; machinist; custodian; nurse's aid; salesperson; licensed practical nurse; accounting clerk or bookkeeper; food-service worker; and computer operator. Funding for classroom training, after a steep drop during the 1980s, has increased in recent years, partly spurred by the effect of the 1988 welfare reform law on JTPA. About a quarter of classroom trainees learned basic educational skills rather than specific occupational training. Job-search training and other forms of brief assistance usually involve two weeks or less of aid. On-the-job training involves a reimbursement to private-sector employers for up to half of the trainee's wages. Finally, a small number of JTPA enrollees are placed in work experience programs. The rationale for the program is the same as that for on-the-job training, that the best form of training is by doing, but the trainees work for government or nonprofit agencies whose wage costs are fully subsidized.

The Job Corps, JTPA's second largest component, assists primarily poor, teenage high school dropouts who are likely to join the ranks of the working poor. Established more than a quarter of a century ago, the Job Corps has weathered criticism of its high costs. It is now widely recognized for its effectiveness in training youngsters with an average of seventh-grade reading skills. The use of residential facilities designed to remove teenagers from their presumably debilitating environments accounts for the huge costs of nearly $20,000 (1992 dollars) per training year. Job Corps enrollees receive intensive vocational and educational training for an average of eight months, and its instructional techniques have served as models for other school and training programs. The Job Corps has recently begun to test its program at nonresidential centers in two cities.

JTPA's dislocated worker program focuses assistance on individuals displaced by foreign economic competition or technological change. About a quarter of the program's participants come from poor or low-income households. Appropriations for 1992 were nearly double the amount they had been in fiscal 1989, enabling program administrators to provide additional participants with classroom training (38 percent in 1991 versus about 30 percent in 1987), although more than two-fifths still receive job-search or other forms of marginal assistance.

JTPA's investment in on-the-job training is problematic. On-the-job training as administered may be providing windfall benefits to employers who take advantage of the subsidy. One study found that three-fifths of the employers who received on-the-job training subsidies stated that they would have hired the same workers even without the inducement. The U.S. General Accounting Office found numerous examples of individuals assigned to on-the-job training who already possessed experience in the particular field, and of contracts for 3.5 months of training in such rudimentary jobs as food-service worker, laborer, and custodian.[5]

Virtually every study of job-search assistance has concluded that the token training has at best short-term benefits. The impact generally dissipates within one to two years because job search does nothing to increase educational or occupational skills. Welfare recipients appear to be the only group to garner longer-term benefits from job-search assistance, probably because it induces some of them to enter the work force.

Evaluations indicate that employment and training programs enhance the earnings and employment of participants, although the effects are modest because the training is brief and inadequate to overcome long-term deficiencies. Quality classroom training has a proven record in enhancing graduates' employment rates and earnings. However, in order to serve more individuals with limited funds, the average duration of actual classroom training programs is only a few months. But widespread recognition of the need for more intensive training, and in some cases additional money, has led in recent years to longer classroom training courses.

Preliminary findings of a JTPA Title IIA evaluation found that only women older than aged 22 experienced statistically significant earnings-gains of 7 percent more than nonparticipants. Out-of-school teenagers and young adults earned less than comparable nonparticipants, but the reduction was statistically significant only for men.[6] The overall results are especially discouraging because participation in the study by local programs was voluntary, and the sample likely reflects JTPA programs with a better-than-average performance. However, various problems with the evaluation cloud interpretation of the results, which should be regarded as tentative.[7]

Vocational Rehabilitation

In 1990 one of nine poor workers had a disability that impeded work. Of the 4.1 million disabled poor of working age, three-fourths reported that they were too disabled to work at all, and three-fifths of the remainder worked at some time during the year. In addition to their physical or mental disabilities, the disabled poor also share the same limited educational attainment levels as other poor workers.

Federally financed vocational rehabilitation for civilians dates back to 1921. The current program provides services to the disabled regardless of income, but priority must be accorded to severely disabled applicants who are potentially able to work. The program does not collect information on the personal or family income of enrollees, but the patterns of service to less educated and minority individuals suggest that the disabled poor often participate, probably because they are more likely to apply for help than the disabled nonpoor.[8]

Because of public sympathy toward the disabled, the rehabilitation program did not suffer budget reductions in the 1980s. In fact, in 1986, Congress stipulated that its appropriations be adjusted annually for inflation. Excluding a few minor programs, the federal government supplies 80 percent of total funding for vocational rehabilitation, with the states matching the remaining 20 percent.

In 1992 the federal government appropriated $2 billion for the program. The funds were inadequate to serve all the disabled, requiring administrators to spread the program's resources thinly. In 1990 the program served 950,000 of the 1.6 million nonworking disabled individuals who were able to work, but less than half of the enrollees obtained education or training.

The U.S. General Accounting Office tracked the earnings patterns of 1980 program graduates who were considered "rehabilitated." Three of every four had worked in 1980, but by 1988 the proportion of 1980 graduates who worked dropped to three of every five. The inflation-adjusted earnings of rehabilated workers rose by a quarter from 1981 to 1988, although some of this increase may be an artifact of low earners dropping out of the work force. But even with the increase, two-fifths of the rehabilitated workers in 1988 earned less than the equivalent of the federal minimum hourly wage for full-time, year-round work.

Vocational rehabilitation accounts for less than 5 percent of total government expenditures for the disabled, which is dominated by cash assistance. Most cash-assistance programs require applicants to prove that they are incapable of work, which may discourage them from pursuing rehabilitation.

Knocking Down Other Barriers

Inadequate skills are not the only barriers to well-paying jobs. Discrimination can relegate minorities, women, and the disabled to low-paying jobs or unemployment. Between the mid-1960s and the end of the following decade, the federal government took increasingly vigorous action to promote equal employment opportunity. In recent years, the federal government has expended efforts on behalf of the disabled, but relaxed enforcement of equal employment opportunity laws and programs for women and minorities. Miscellaneous other obstacles, especially a lack of affordable childcare, also limit employment.

Combating Discrimination

Discrimination remains a significant barrier to employment, although pinpointing its extent and impact is elusive because bigotry is now practiced more insidiously than prior to the passage of civil rights legislation. In 1990, despite hard-fought progress, women, minorities, and the disabled were disproportionately found among the working poor (Figure 12).

Progress in securing greater employment and high wages has been uneven among these groups, with women making the most headway and the disabled making the least. Until the 1980s women faced higher unemployment rates than men, but in the early 1990s men experienced slightly higher unemployment rates than women. Weekly earnings of women employed full-time had

Figure 12. Minorities and the disabled are more concentrated among poor workers than they are in the entire work force (1990).

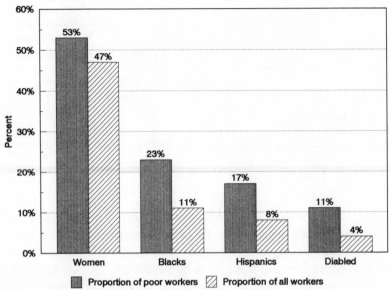

Source: U.S. Census Bureau

remained at 60 percent of the earnings of men for decades, but in recent years have risen to 74 percent. These gains are partly attributable to the fact that young female work-force entrants now match their male counterparts in educational attainment. Nonetheless, in 1990, 25- to 34-year old women who worked full-time, year-round still earned only 77 percent as much as men (Table 7).

As blatant discrimination against women has receded, much of the persistent earnings gap is probably attributable to women's child-rearing. After accounting for age, education, and other factors, prime-age, childless, white female workers earned 91 percent as much as men, compared to 72 percent for mothers.[9] The earnings disadvantage of mothers is partly due to the fact that time spent out of the labor force decreases their work experience, but, even after accounting for job tenure, women still earn less than men. Many employers tend to view motherhood as conflicting with employment responsibilities.

Race bias remains a more serious problem. Unemployment rates

Table 7. Female high school graduates 25 to 34 years old still earn less than men with less than a high school education (1990)

Education	Men	Women	Ratio of women to men
Total	$27,743	$21,337	76.9%
4 or more years college	36,909	28,692	77.7
1–3 years college	28,298	20,872	73.8
4 years high school	24,038	17,076	71.0
1–3 years high school	19,453	13,385	68.8

Source: U.S. Census Bureau

of blacks are more than double those of whites, and the gap has risen in the past two decades. Weekly earnings of full-time black workers grew substantially relative to those of white ones between 1967 and 1978, rising from 70 to 80 percent of average earnings of white workers, but the ratio fell to 78 percent by 1991. The 1990 annual earnings of 25- to 34-year-old full-time, year-round workers suggests that black men experience the largest earnings gap compared with whites, and that the Hispanic/white earnings gap is generally explained by Hispanics' lower educational attainment (Table 8). Young black men with four years of high school earn less than white dropouts. Paradoxically, the position of blacks in the labor market has deteriorated compared with that of whites, although black student test scores have risen relative to white ones in the past two decades.

More direct measures of discrimination reinforce the evidence derived from unemployment and earnings disparities. The use of "testers," which has provided powerful evidence of housing discrimination, has recently been applied to job bias. White and minority applicants were provided with identical résumés, matched by physical appearance as closely as possible, and coached to give identical answers to questions. They were then sent to apply for the same job openings. Although matching job applicants is considerably more difficult than matching house- or apartment-hunters, tests of entry-level jobs typically filled by

Table 8. Full-time, year-round 25- to 34-year-old black workers earn much less than white ones with similar educational attainments (1990)

	Men		Women	
	Black/ White	Hispanic/ White	Black/ White	Hispanic/ White
Total	73%	74%	85%	80%
4 years college	74	89	91	86
1–3 years college	84	88	91	94
4 years high school	78	83	88	93
1–3 years high school	73	88	NA	88

Source: U.S. Census Bureau

high school graduates demonstrated widespread bias. Employers made job offers to whites more frequently than to blacks and Hispanics.[10]

	Matching of	
Offer made to	*blacks and whites*	*Hispanics and whites*
White applicant	44%	43%
Both applicants	41	41
Minority applicant	15	16

If anything, the tests underestimated the prevalence of bias, because only positions listed in the want ads were tested (nonadvertising employers are more likely to discriminate), and the analysts excluded instances where one of the matched applicants was screened out via telephone before a face-to-face contact occurred.

The federal government took halting steps in the 1940s to combat racial job discrimination, but not until the 1960s did all three federal branches broadly challenge discriminatory employment practices:

1. The 1963 Equal Pay Act requires that men and women receive equal pay for equal work.

2. Title VII of the 1964 Civil Rights Act proscribes employment discrimination on the basis of race, gender, religion, or national origin.

3. Executive order 11246, issued by President Johnson in 1965, requires federal contractors to implement affirmative-action plans.

4. The 1967 Age Discrimination in Employment Act bans discrimination against workers aged 40 or older.

5. The 1990 Americans with Disabilities Act bans employment discrimination on the basis of physical or mental disability. The law also bans discrimination in public accommodations and transportation, which will also facilitate employment.

6. The 1991 Civil Rights Act, which is discussed below.

In addition to federal actions, vigorous antibias laws or programs have been instituted by many states and private employers.

Antidiscrimination efforts in the 1960s focused on the hiring and promotion processes, an approach that can reduce but not necessarily prohibit bias. For example, an employer may fulfill the letter of the law by soliciting and considering applications from minorities, but never actually hiring one. For this reason, in the 1970s the federal government, especially the Supreme Court, placed more emphasis on affirmative-action results instead of intent and process. Until the 1980s the Equal Employment Opportunity Commission aggressively pursued antidiscriminatory policies, based partly on the Court's decisions.

Federal equal opportunity policy changed significantly during the 1980s. The Reagan administration limited enforcement to flagrant violations by requiring that intent to discriminate be established before the government intervened, and it rejected numerical affirmative-action goals. By the decade's end the Equal Employment Opportunity Commission was less than half as successful as in 1980 at achieving settlements of discrimination cases, and almost twice as likely to reject bias complaints. The Justice Department waged an even more activist policy against previous legislative, regulatory, and judicial interpretations of equal opportunity rules by challenging them in the courts.

In 1989 the Supreme Court reversed previous judicial interpretations and endorsed many of the equal employment policies of the Reagan and Bush administrations. The 1991 Civil Rights Act limited or reversed several 1989 Supreme Court decisions, and it covers a broad variety of antibias issues. A product of compromise accommodating opposing viewpoints, the new law is ambiguous on some key points that are likely to be adjudicated by the courts. Major provisions include:

1. Victims of job discrimination based on gender, disability, and religion can for the first time collect compensatory or punitive damages (minorities previously could do so), but only in cases where intentional discrimination is proved.
2. In cases where discriminatory intent is not established, individuals can nonetheless charge discrimination (*a*) if a practice adversely affects employees on the basis of race, color, gender, national origin, or religion and (*b*) if the employer cannot provide adequate evidence that the practice is job-related and consistent with business necessity. The latter provision returns the burden of proof to employers, reversing a 1989 Supreme Court decision.
3. Racial bias after hiring is prohibited, reversing another 1989 Court decision that limited remedies for posthiring discrimination.
4. "Race-norming," a practice used by some private-sector and government employers to artificially boost minorities' scores in hiring tests, is banned.

The 1990 Americans with Disabilities Act was the most significant expansion of civil rights law in a quarter-century. Its employment provisions prohibit discrimination against the disabled in all employment practices, from hiring to firing, although employers with fewer than fifteen employees are exempt from the law. Employers must also make reasonable efforts to enable qualified disabled applicants to gain access and to perform on a job. The employment provisions became effective for employers with twenty-five or more employees in July 1992, and companies with fifteen to twenty-four workers must comply two years later.

Equal employment opportunity laws, administrative policies, and court decisions have unquestionably reduced discrimination, although the effects have been uneven.[11] Job discrimination remains a significant factor preventing workers from escaping poverty. This is demonstrated by employment and earnings disparities, direct tests of matched job applicants, and the concentration of minority groups among poor workers. The 1991 Civil Rights Act and the 1990 Americans with Disabilities Act may potentially reduce job bias, but will require vigilant enforcement. One additional enforcement mechanism that would likely prove both highly effective and acceptable to the public is the use of matched job applicants. Congress endorsed the use of testers in the 1988 Federal Fair Housing Act amendments to monitor compliance and enforce the law.

Childcare

Lack of accessible or affordable childcare can limit or preclude employment. This is especially true for the poor, whose net earnings after childcare and other work-related expenses may leave little additional income. In 1990, slightly more than half of poor workers had children. Two-fifths of working-poor parents or other adults in the household cited home responsibilities as the main reason they did not work a full year in 1990, and half of parents or other adults in the household who did not work at all during the year offered the same explanation. Family responsibilities far outweigh any other single reason given by poor adults for not working. In 1986 a third of poor mothers in their twenties reported that they would seek paid work if affordable childcare were available.[12]

Less than half of working-poor parents use childcare, because typically only one adult works in two-parent poor families. Because of their impoverishment, in 1987 only a quarter of the 1.4 million working-poor parents who used childcare paid for it; the remainder relied on relatives. In 1990 working-poor parents with preschoolers who paid for childcare spent a fourth of the total family income on it. This financial burden—which approaches the limit of what families should pay for a major expense such as housing—is a telling indication of the obstacles poor parents face in expanding paid work time without affordable childcare.

Since the mid-1980s the federal government has become increasingly responsive to the childcare needs of poor parents. Head Start combines childcare assistance for poor workers with an enriched educational environment for preschoolers. The program stresses the latter, but the program also serves as a childcare provider for half of Head Start working parents. Between 1989 and 1992, inflation-adjusted Head Start funding rose by more than 50 percent, to $2.2 billion. In 1991 nearly 600,000 children enrolled, roughly 30 percent of poor children aged 3 to 5. In 1992

Congress boosted, at President Bush's proposal, an additional $600 million for Head Start for 1993. In recent years public schools have also become important providers of childcare, although data on the poverty status of school enrollees are not available.

In addition to enabling poor parents to work at least part-time, Head Start helps to minimize future poverty of the enrollees. However, the program possesses some drawbacks from the perspective of working parents. Only 6 percent of Head Start children are in full-day programs lasting nine hours, and virtually all programs shut down during the summer. Thus most working parents must combine Head Start with other childcare arrangements. In addition, the program relies heavily on volunteer help from parents of participants. Therefore, Head Start parents who work draw upon the program's supply of free labor, and if an adequate supply of volunteers were not available program costs would rise.

The social services block grant (Title XX of the Social Security Act) provides another important source of childcare for the working poor. The $2.8 billion annual grant can be used by local communities for a wide variety of purposes. Congress has more or less frozen the social-services block grant since 1972, and consequently inflation-adjusted annual funding has declined by two-thirds. In 1988 the states devoted about $450 million of Title XX funds to childcare, but the share spent on childcare for poor workers is unknown.

The 1990 Omnibus Budget Reconciliation Act created two new childcare programs. A childcare block grant began operations in September 1991, with appropriations of $732 million for fiscal 1991, and $825 million for the following year. Eligibility is restricted to parents who are working or attending school or training programs, and whose income falls below 75 percent of the state's median income. A smaller childcare program, established in October 1990, targets low-income, working parents who are at risk of becoming welfare recipients. The states may obtain up to $300 million in federal funds each year, but must match federal funds with their own contributions, at the Medicaid matching rate formula. The programs are of recent origin, and little is known about the operations of either. The same is true of the Even Start Family Literacy program, created in 1988 and funded at $70 million in fiscal 1992. The program is similar to Head Start, but it serves a broader age range of children from birth to age 7 and teaches literacy to their parents.

In 1991 federal tax breaks for childcare amounted to an estimated $3.1 billion, benefiting 6 million families. Because the 1986 Tax Reform Act virtually eliminated federal income taxes for the poor, only an estimated 14,000 families with incomes below $10,000 used the credit, and their average claim was less than $50. If the childcare credit were made refundable, it could be an important benefit for the working poor.

In just a few years, the federal government has improved the availability of childcare for poor workers and thereby enhanced their opportunities for seeking employment. State-funded extensions of kindergarten and prekindergarten schooling in recent decades, although not intended as childcare, have done even more. A new federal childcare assistance program for welfare recipients (discussed in chapter 7) encourages the nonworking poor to enter the labor force. However, poor parents require further help to secure employment, and a major drawback of the new programs is that the fragmentation of childcare assistance is not only administratively inefficient but also makes it difficult for poor parents to find help.

Are the Walls Crumbling Down?

A significant number of adult Americans lack the basic educational and vocational skills necessary for productive and sustained employment that would raise their earnings above the poverty threshold. The key to assisting these individuals lies in strengthening both the basic and second-chance education systems. Those who leave school without acquiring basic skills are likely to have low incomes, be subject to intermittent spells of forced idleness, and become dependent on welfare. Federally funded second-chance opportunities fill a gap in the education and training system, as well as ameliorate the problems of the employable poor. There is also a need for more vigorous enforcement of equal employment opportunity laws.

The emphasis on federal policies should not obscure the need for businesses, unions, and state and local governments to work toward removing barriers to employment. Employers can provide skill training and voluntarily promote equal employment opportunity. States and localities, which administer most of the federal second-chance programs, also have primary responsibility for the funding and quality of the education system. In addition, although the working poor are often victims, their own actions are crucial for improving their skills and avoiding dysfunctional behavior. Many are failed by the school system and the labor markets, but others fail school or lack the self-discipline and motivation to find a niche in the workplace. A combined and concerted effort on the part of all involved would improve workers' basic skills and lower other barriers to employment.

6. *Finding and Creating Jobs*

Complementing efforts to knock down employment barriers, the federal government attempts to match job seekers with suitable job openings and to increase the number of jobs. Many jobs remain vacant because institutions designed to match job openings with individuals seeking work fall short of carrying out their mission. Although the U.S. economy has generated many new jobs, it has not created enough for all job seekers.

The federal-state employment (or job) service attempts to match available job seekers with vacant positions. The Wagner-Peyser Act established the employment service agency in 1933 during the Great Depression. The federal government also offers a tax break, the targeted jobs tax credit, to employers who hire disadvantaged applicants, primarily poor youth and welfare recipients. The rationale for the program is that employers will be more likely to hire disadvantaged applicants because the tax break compensates for the added training costs and presumed lower productivity of individuals who may be less qualified than other job applicants. The tax break is supposed to give low-income applicants an edge over more advantaged applicants.

The job service and tax credit probably only marginally increase total employment. To directly increase the number of jobs, the federal government financed job creation programs, especially during the 1930s and 1970s. The last major effort was abandoned during the mid-1980s, but the government still funds several small programs for teenagers and young adults, older workers, and Native Americans.

The Employment Service

Filling job vacancies expeditiously benefits employers and job seekers, as well as society. Employers reap savings when operations are not interrupted due to an inadequate supply of employees, and workers benefit from steady earnings. Society benefits from greater tax revenue, as well as lower welfare outlays and unemployment insurance payments to the jobless. Private employment agencies almost exclusively serve employers and job seekers who can afford the fees. Consequently, a formal and free job-matching service is essential for low-wage and unskilled workers.

Changing federal mandates have pulled the job service in a variety of different, sometimes conflicting, directions, without greater funding to meet its added responsibilities. Adjusted for inflation, job service appropriations have declined by 40 percent from a peak of $1.4 billion in 1979 to $822 million in 1992. Following severe cuts in 1981, on the eve of the most severe recession since the Great Depression, public employment offices nationwide declined from 2,600 in 1980 to 2,000 in 1992. Not surprisingly, the proportion of job seekers who received employment service assistance has dropped from 31 to 23 percent during the last two decades.

Decreased assistance to the disadvantaged has exacerbated the problems caused by reduced financing. Between 1978 and 1990, the share of the employment service clientele that was economically disadvantaged applicants fell by half, from 29 to 14 percent, and the share of the clientele made up of unemployment-insurance recipients, who are usually not poor, grew from 23 to 37 percent. The drop in aid to the poor is partly due to federal creation of new employment and training programs for Aid to Families with Dependent Children (AFDC) and food-stamp recipients, many of whom were formerly required to register with the job service. The new programs could use the employment service, but most have not. Administrators of Job Training Partnership Act (JTPA) programs have criticized public employment service offices, and JTPA performance standards that require a specified proportion of participants to obtain jobs made referrals to the job service by local JTPA programs even less likely. Local JTPA administrators tend to apply the standards to contractors, who prefer to place participants themselves rather than rely upon public employment offices in which they have little confidence.

In the 1960s the federal government required that the job service give special attention to the needs of poor job seekers. However, since 1982 federal oversight of the program has virtually vanished. Although Congress rejected Reagan administration proposals to turn the employment service over to the states, the U.S. Labor Department implemented this policy administratively by an 80 percent cut in its oversight staff to twenty employees, where it remains currently. The U.S. General Accounting Office has characterized federal reviews of state administration as a "meaningless exercise."[1]

During fiscal 1990 a little more than half of the 19.2 million individuals who applied for assistance at public employment offices received at least some service. To qualify for unemployment insurance benefits, claimants are required to apply, but need not seek help after that. Since 1984, public employment offices have referred between 7 million to 8 million individuals annually to job openings listed with the offices by employers. In 1990, 43 percent (3.2 million) of those referred were hired. Half of the hirings were for temporary jobs expected to last less than five months.

The last major evaluation of the employment service occurred in 1980–81. The analysts concluded that women, but not men, who obtained employment service job referrals subsequently experienced higher incomes. Overall, benefits garnered exceeded program costs by two to one.[2] The findings demonstrate the potential value of the job service, although the program has significantly contracted since the study was conducted.

Technological advances have dramatically enhanced the potential usefulness of the employment service. The matching of job seekers' interests and abilities with suitable job openings is a task tailor-made for computers, saving staff time for instruction in job search techniques, résumé preparation, and other assistance that enhances job-seeking success by applicants. Concerned that they would be swamped with unsuitable referrals, many employers have long hesitated to list job openings with public employment offices. If applicants were properly screened, employers might be more receptive to referrals. With the implementation of such safeguards, Congress might consider requiring all employers to list openings with public employment offices. This reform would necessitate a substantial initial investment, but should be highly cost effective in the long run.

A perennial controversy exists whether the employment service should target its services primarily to the disadvantaged. The unemployed use a variety of methods in their job hunts, including personal contacts, newspaper advertisements, and private and public employment agencies. Slightly less than one in ten job seekers finds employment through the public employment service. Should the public employment service compete with private employment agencies, coordinate with these agencies, or pursue a separate market niche?

If the employment service improves the quality of its job listings and its applicants, its reputation will be enhanced, but its service to the disadvantaged may suffer. However, if it continues to serve mostly low-skilled workers, the job vacancies that employers report to the agency will continue to be of low quality.

Sharp criticism of the employment service may arise in part from unrealistic expectations. Most individuals find jobs through informal networks rather than institutional arrangements. An appropriate measure of the employment service's utility is whether it plays a beneficial role, however limited, in helping job seekers. As long as there are employers who search for workers in a haphazard fashion, and as long as there are employees who cannot find suitable jobs on their own, the employment service will be needed to bring them together. A comprehensive system is of vital importance to the working poor, who are much less likely than more advantaged job seekers to find unlisted openings. With the brunt of routine job-matching performed by computer, professional employment service staff could concentrate on teaching the disadvantaged job search skills.

Short of wholesale reform, the federal government urgently needs to bolster direction and funding for the program. A recent U.S. General Accounting Office study concluded that public employment offices with the highest job placement and wage results set measurable performance goals and reinforced them with monitoring and rewards and that they emphasized client services, including individualized attention for job seekers and rapid responses to employer requests. The study's findings are worth careful consideration and perhaps implementation.

Targeted Jobs Tax Credit

Spawned in an era of experimentation in the 1970s, wage subsidies reflect classical economic theory—to increase the demand for goods (or workers), lower the price. Congress expected that subsidies would not only compensate employers for the perceived low productivity of the poor but also help the disadvantaged overcome the prejudice they often confront in seeking employment.

Although theoretically appealing, jobs tax credits have proved disappointing in practice. Enacted in 1978, the Targeted Jobs Tax Credit (TJTC) offers a tax credit to employers who hire targeted individuals. The credit amounts to 40 percent of the first $6,000 wages during the initial year of employment. Employers are entitled to receive the credit for hiring:

1. Individuals aged 18 to 22, Vietnam veterans, and ex-felons living in low-income households;
2. AFDC, Supplemental Security Income (for the aged poor, blind, and disabled), and state or local general assistance recipients; and
3. Disabled individuals undergoing vocational rehabilitation.

In addition, employers are entitled to subsidies of 40 percent of the first $3,000 paid in wages to low-income 16- and 17-year-olds hired for summer jobs.

A Troubled Program

The federal government has restricted TJTC eligibility since its inception and reduced the regular credit's value by 75 percent after inflation. Moreover, in each of the past five years the federal government has severely hampered the operations of TJTC by either letting its legislative authorization lapse or reauthorizing it just before the expiration date. Consequently, the number of certified TJTC workers dropped from a peak of 622,000 in 1985 to 452,000 in 1991.

Even in TJTC's relative heyday, employers sought the credit much less often than might be expected, given that certifications

Figure 13. Youth and welfare recipients account for most TJTC certifications (1991).

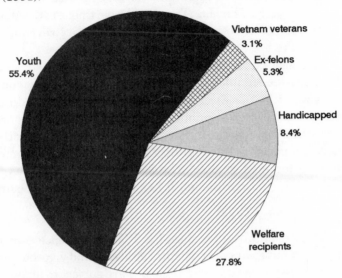

Source: U.S. Labor Department

have been easy to acquire. A pilot project in the late 1970s found that most employers were uninterested in hiring disadvantaged youth. Offered a 100 percent wage subsidy, hiring and firing discretion, and no responsibility for benefit costs, wage disbursement, and tax withholding, less than a fifth of employers approached agreed to hire any disadvantaged teenager.[3] The results suggest that applicants' skill deficiencies or employer bias present more of a barrier than wage costs.

Despite its diminished size, TJTC plays a significant labor market role for young adults and welfare recipients, who together account for more than 80 percent of total tax credits (Figure 13). In 1990 roughly a sixth of all low-income workers aged 18 to 22 were certified.

Given the clientele, TJTC employees work at low-skilled, low-paid jobs. The U.S. General Accounting Office found that 59 percent of the 650 participating firms were retail stores and restaurants. In 1990 three-fourths of all certifications were for service or clerical occupations. In 1991 slightly more than one-third of TJTC hirees earned $4.25 per hour or less. Only 9 percent earned more than $7 per hour. The 1991 increase in the hourly minimum wage from $3.80 to $4.25 undoubtedly boosted the earnings of TJTC workers. The U.S. Treasury Department estimated that in 1991 the credit cost $245 million in lost tax revenue, but the figures are not much better than guesses.

Evidence exists that employers who obtained tax credits would have hired a significant proportion of the same individuals in the absence of TJTC. Employers can legally submit credit requests for *all* new hirees to public employment offices on or before the date they begin work. But applying for the credit after the hiring decision negates the program's intent of increasing employment for the targeted groups.[4] The federal government has failed to redress this flaw, although it has been repeatedly documented.

Strengthening TJTC

Despite its initial promise, the TJTC experience demonstrates that without clear governmental guidance and vigorous oversight, private-sector antipoverty remedies are subject to abuse. TJTC is doubly vulnerable because it cannot function properly without an efficient employment service, which has been hobbled. Throughout its tenure, the Reagan administration attempted to abolish TJTC, and the Bush administration has replaced this opposition with nothing better than neglect. The U.S. Labor Department has ignored TJTC's serious deficiencies, and Congress has done little to fulfill its oversight responsibilities. Consequently, TJTC has largely become a business subsidy rather than an antipoverty program.

The hiring of individuals who would have been employed anyway could be addressed by requiring employers, subject to appropriate penalties, to certify that the individuals were hired after the voucher request. If the employment service were strengthened, it could exercise more effective verification of TJTC claims. In addition, simultaneously raising the $6,000 current wage base and lowering the credit rate below 40 percent should have some effect in deemphasizing the credit for the lowest paid jobs. In 1992 the $6,000 wage base was a third lower than the earnings from a full-time, year-round, minimum-wage job.

TJTC may be an experiment worth retaining, but only if the

necessary reforms are implemented. Sadly, neither Congress nor the Bush administration has demonstrated the slightest inclination to fulfill its responsibilities.

Job Creation

Once a matter of pressing concern, the plight of the jobless has been shunted aside because of indifference, pejorative attitudes toward jobs creation programs, and the federal budget deficit. The federal government has mounted jobs programs following every downturn of the past three decades, except for the recent recession. The last major jobs program expired in the mid-1980s, although several small efforts continue. In the recent recession, the federal government supplied additional unemployment benefits, but these primarily assist individuals who are relatively better off than the working poor. Ironically, recent support for jobs programs has emanated from the conservatives who castigated the programs of the 1970s. Requiring recipients to work in return for welfare benefits—commonly called workfare—necessitates public job creation.

Ongoing Programs

The largest remaining jobs programs serve the youngest and oldest individuals in the work force. The summer youth employment program authorizes project administrators to offer participants a variety of services, but in practice enrollees are given jobs. The average participant works thirty-two hours weekly for seven weeks at a government agency, school, or nonprofit organization. Local program administrators are required to assess the reading and math skills of enrollees and allocate at least some funding to teaching the three Rs. Individuals aged 14 to 21 are eligible, but only one of every five enrollees is aged 18 or older, and two of every five enrollees are aged 14 or 15. The summer jobs program peaked in 1978, with a $1.4 billion (1992 dollars) appropriation and 1 million enrollees; the 1992 appropriation was $683 million, and 554,000 youth participated in 1991. Presidents Reagan and Bush repeatedly attempted to eliminate the summer employment program and transfer its funds to a year-round youth program.

Reacting to the May 1992 Los Angeles riots, Congress appropriated an additional $500 million for the 1992 summer program to fund 360,000 jobs.

The federal college work-study program, established by the 1964 Economic Opportunity Act, provided part-time jobs to 703,000 students during the 1990–91 school year at a cost of $615 million in fiscal 1992. By law, participating schools must supply 30 percent of work-study funding, but the match need not be in cash.

Federal postsecondary aid is supposed to help financially needy students, but eligibility is defined more broadly than for most low-income programs. In order to include private schools in the program, financial need is determined on the basis of the student's (or family's) income, assets, and the cost of attendance. Thus a middle- or even upper-income student can qualify for college work-study at an expensive school. Consequently, during the 1990–91 school year only one-fifth of dependent undergraduate work-study enrollees came from families with less than $12,000 annual income, and two-fifths of enrollees came from families with annual incomes above $30,000. College work-study jobs should emphasize the needs of disadvantaged students who are less likely to be hired elsewhere and need greater financial help than other students to stay in school.

Most work-study positions involve clerical or low-skilled jobs on campus, including word processing, filing, answering telephones, and kitchen work. The program spreads the funds thinly in order to hire as many students as possible. For example, even full-time students were paid an average of $1,000 during the 1990–91 school year. Even if no job pays more than the federal minimum wage, the program would provide each participant with 250 hours of work.

The senior community-service employment program, a product of the 1960s antipoverty efforts, is the only remaining adult public-service jobs program. Individuals aged 55 or older who live in households with incomes below 125 percent of the poverty line are eligible for part-time jobs; three of every five enrollees are aged 65 or older. Probably because of the political potency of the elderly community, the program was one of the few employment and training programs to escape budget cuts in the early 1980s. The 1992 appropriation of $395 million was sufficient for about 65,000 job slots. Most participants work in recreation centers and parks, social-service agencies, schools, or nutrition agencies for the elderly. Participants remain in the program much longer than those enrolled in other government employment programs. The median stay is almost a year, but because some continue for much longer the mean duration is nearly two years. Slightly more than a fifth of those leaving the seniors' program obtain unsubsidized jobs.

Hourly wages for the summer-youth, college work-study, and the seniors' jobs programs are tied to the federal minimum wage. Without additional funding, these programs were obliged to reduce job slots or work time when the statutory minimum hourly wage rose from $3.35 to $4.25 during 1990 and 1991. If the summer jobs program paid less than the minimum wage to those aged 14 or 15, more teenagers could be hired.

The federal government also continues to fund two smaller jobs programs. The Economic Development Administration finances public-works jobs. The program peaked at more than $1 billion (1992 dollars) in 1978, and dropped to $227 million in 1992 after repeated presidential attempts to eliminate it. The agency collects little information on program operations.

Employment programs for Native Americans, funded under JTPA at $75 million in 1992, also provide some subsidized jobs. Congress continued its support for public service employment on reservations because job shortages there could not be ameliorated by the private sector alone.[5]

Forsaken Too Soon

Despite rhetorical adherence to the work ethic, the government devotes far more resources to cash payments for the jobless and employable poor than to helping them earn a living. Indeed, rigid employment restrictions for welfare and disability assistance recipients discourage beneficiaries from working.

Although some argue that joblessness is due more to individual choice than to job shortages, this view is belied by the evidence of past full employment periods and by empirical studies. For example, one social experiment conducted in the late 1970s examined the feasibility of guaranteeing jobs for poor youth, a group often singled out as lacking a work ethic. These poor youth responded en masse to a job offer. In the seventeen participating communities, four-fifths of eligible youth who learned of the program applied, and three-fifths of all eligible youth participated.

Public job creation serves four separate but overlapping needs:

1. The programs, of course, alleviate joblessness, hardship, and poverty.
2. If sufficiently large, the expenditures can help the local or national economy emerge from a recession.
3. Providing jobs to able-bodied welfare recipients is a necessary complement to a welfare system, promoting the work ethic and self-sufficiency.
4. Jobs programs produce needed services that are otherwise neglected.[6]

Although all of these elements contribute vitally to the nation's economic and social health, from the perspective of poor workers the most important elements are the impact of jobs programs in alleviating joblessness and poverty.

The federal government first enacted jobs programs to alleviate the ravages of the Great Depression during the 1930s, employing as many as 4.6 million workers at a time. The accomplishments of the New Deal work programs demonstrated conclusively the value of the undertaking. The Public Works Adminstration built or assisted in building some of the largest and best-known public works in the United States, including the Grand Coulee Dam. The Work Projects Administration built 617,000 miles of new roads, and built or repaired 124,000 bridges and viaducts, 120,000 public buildings, and 30,000 stadiums, parks, playgrounds, and athletic fields.

For nearly two decades after World War II (the New Deal jobs programs were shut down during the war), the federal government funded no direct job creation. Following the 1962 enactment of a public-works jobs program, funding for job creation escalated rapidly in the mid-1970s to a peak of nearly $25 billion (1992 dollars), which directly created more than a million full-time equivalent jobs and indirectly created many more. The subsidized jobs entailed two traditional governmental functions: providing

Figure 14. At their peak in the late 1970s, job creation programs significantly reduced unemployment.

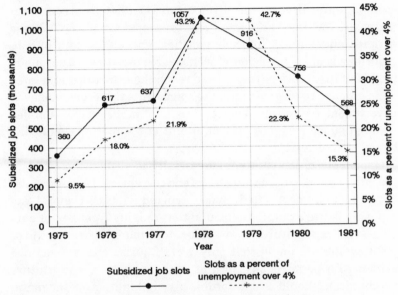

Source: U.S. Congressional Research Service, *The Comprehensive Employment and Training Act: A Compilation of Data,* pp. 6–7, 12–13.

services and constructing public facilities. However, jobs programs contracted almost as suddenly as they had expanded. Ironically, the federal government eliminated the public-service employment program in 1981 just as the nation entered the worst recession since the Great Depression.

The disillusionment with job creation programs is due to misconceptions that they do little to alleviate joblessness, are exorbitantly expensive, and are inherently vulnerable to waste and fraud. When adequately funded in the late 1970s, job creation programs significantly reduced unemployment. An appropriate performance indicator is to gauge the share of unemployment reduced above a target of 4 percent. By this standard, employment programs at their height reduced the job deficit by 43 percent (Figure 14).

The costs of a jobs program are often cited as an argument against the undertaking. Yet the price of inaction is compelling, even if it does not fully appear as a line item in the federal budget.

Rising unemployment rates have demonstrated a correlation with increased social-program outlays, mortality, health impairments, crime, mental illness, and divorce rates. Although precise estimates are lacking, the costs of jobs programs are mitigated, and perhaps outweighed, by their benefits. The wages paid by jobs programs replace a portion of welfare disbursements and unemployment insurance payments and reduce health-care and related costs. Subject to income taxes, the wages directly return money to government treasuries. The services and public works supplied through subsidized jobs provide useful and sometimes enduring benefits to society.

Opponents of job creation successfully identified the effort in the public mind with incompetence and corruption. However, relatively little demonstrated abuse occurred. A U.S. General Accounting Office examination found that roughly 2 percent of public-service expenditures were subject to fraud or abuse.[7] A major 1979 evaluation found that only 1 of 42 jurisdictions examined evidenced a persistent pattern of mismanagement.[8] Any future jobs program should be extraordinarily vigilant to gain and maintain public trust, and stringent safeguards will be necessary to prevent mismanagement. Past mistakes justify improving—not abjuring—future efforts.

Future jobs programs should target primarily the long-term jobless, the low-income population, and job-ready welfare recipients. There is no shortage of useful work that could be performed to fulfill needs unmet by the market economy; society's work is never done. The limited skills of many employable poor individuals would dovetail well with such tasks as teacher aides, childcare providers, and long-term-care providers, which already rely heavily on unskilled, low-wage labor.

Not Much Help

In the 1980s the federal government sharply curtailed employment service and job creation efforts. Although the employment service places millions of workers each year, there is widespread agreement that it needs considerable reform and strengthening. The Targeted Jobs Tax Credit has existed for a decade and a half, but its value to poor workers remains questionable. Job creation programs have been all but abandoned, even in the face of recessionary hardship. Although most workers find jobs without federal assistance, the government has a significant role to play in helping the disadvantaged find employment.

7. Linking Welfare with Work

Earlier chapters examined policies that promote economic self-sufficiency by raising the earnings of low-paid workers, funding skill-training programs, helping the unemployed find jobs, and creating jobs for those who cannot find work. These are the best antipoverty measures, because economic self-sufficiency is preferable to reliance on welfare. Society benefits both from the increased output of the poor workers and from lower welfare costs. The goal of public policy should be to ensure sufficient work and earnings so that all who can work are able to escape poverty, thus leaving only the unemployable to rely on welfare.

Equating employment with economic self-sufficiency, many free market advocates argue that any adult who has a job does not need welfare assistance. The existence of poor workers belies this assertion. Disqualifying poor workers from public assistance discourages work effort if welfare is more rewarding than labor. For example, a low-income parent's need for affordable medical care may be sufficiently compelling to forsake work to qualify for Medicaid. Income supplements should be a last but an available resort if the working poor and their families are to obtain the basic necessities of life, and as long as wages are inadequate even for full-time, year-round workers to escape poverty.

In some respects, the welfare and social insurance system operates in a perverse way and is often of scant help to the working poor. Cash assistance to the working poor is frequently negligible. In-kind benefits provide additional aid, but many poor workers are denied these benefits (Figure 15). Nearly half of poor workers

Figure 15. Many government programs are more likely to benefit nonelderly poor households whose head did not work than to assist households with a working head (1989 or 1990).

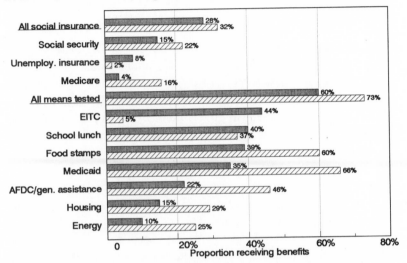

Note: For all social insurance and unemployment insurance, poverty is defined on the basis of family income exclusive of government cash benefits.

Source: U.S. Census Bureau

do not have health insurance and are ineligible for Medicaid. Social insurance programs benefit low-income individuals when they retire, become disabled, or lose their jobs, but not when they are working. Welfare assistance to the working poor has declined because of overall cuts in domestic programs and because specific cuts have reduced aid to poor workers.

This chapter also examines the mounting interest in work programs for welfare recipients. This interest reflects the belief that work improves the long-term prospects of the recipients and that the right to welfare engenders responsibilities to society.

The debate over work incentives and work requirements for welfare recipients has deflected attention away from the welfare system's inadequacies in addressing the needs of the working poor. Poor workers should be eligible to receive welfare and in-kind assistance as a necessary complement to their meager earnings; for them, work and welfare must go together. It is inconsistent to disdain efforts to improve the working conditions of low-wage employees and at the same time support cuts in welfare benefits.

Cash Assistance

Aid to Families with Dependent Children (AFDC), the largest means-tested cash-benefits program, provides assistance to impoverished families with children. About two out of three AFDC recipients are children, and, in nine out of ten AFDC families, the father is absent. The federal government finances more than half of AFDC costs, but individual states establish need and benefit standards and administer the program. Most families do not languish forever of AFDC, and for them the program serves as a temporary income support system. Many families, however, remain on the rolls for years and could benefit from educational, job search, and training assistance. The median continuous length of time spent on AFDC is 2.2 years, but, because many leave the rolls for a period and then return, and because a minority remain for a much longer duration, the estimated mean total time on AFDC rolls per recipient is an estimated 7 years during a lifetime.

In fiscal 1991 federal and state AFDC outlays totaled $21.3 billion and benefited a monthly average of 12.6 million individuals. Total inflation-adjusted expenditures grew until 1973, stabilized through 1977, contracted until 1985, and then grew again after 1989 due to the 1990–91 recession. The number of recipients had remained relatively constant from 1972 until the economic downturn in 1990 spurred a 25 percent rise in the number of recipients to a historic high of 13.6 million in early 1992. However, 60 percent of poor children received AFDC in 1990, as compared to a high of 81 percent in 1973. The average maximum AFDC monthly benefit for a mother and two children, after adjusting for inflation, fell 41 percent from 1972 to 1991. More than four-fifths of AFDC recipients obtain food stamps, which partially offset the fall in AFDC benefits, so the reduction in combined AFDC/food-stamp benefits was 26.5 percent during the period. AFDC payments leave most families in poverty. The maximum AFDC grant varies substantially among states, but a family of three living in the median AFDC state would obtain a maximum combined

AFDC/food-stamp grant worth less than three-fourths of the poverty threshold.

Single-parent families are more likely than two-parent families to qualify for AFDC. Two-parent benefits (called AFDC-unemployed parent) were not available until 1961, a quarter of a century after AFDC became law. The unemployed parent component was optional in nearly half the states until the 1988 Family Support Act made it mandatory. However, the program's expansion has to date had but a modest impact, mostly because the added states tended to have relatively small caseloads and less generous benefits. Only 8.5 percent of the unemployed parent caseload increase is attributable to the 90,000 recipients from the newly added states; Kentucky and Texas accounted for more than half of the increase. The newly added states may also limit unemployed parent benefits to six months out of every thirteen-month period, although these states cannot deny Medicaid coverage. Altogether, in 1991 unemployed parent recipients constituted 9.1 percent of the total AFDC caseload.

Unlike the single parent component, the unemployed parent program's eligibility rules stipulate a work history. To qualify for AFDC, the family's principal earner must have worked in at least six out of thirteen quarters ending within one year before the AFDC application, or else qualify for unemployment insurance, which also requires a work history. Once eligible, the unemployed parent can work up to a hundred hours per month and still receive AFDC. This provision probably has the unintended effect of discouraging work (or at least reported work) above this amount. It also hurts low-paid workers, because some lose AFDC eligibility from the hours limit before being disqualified by the earnings limitation.

AFDC treatment of earned income has oscillated during the past quarter of a century. Until 1967 recipients lost $1 in welfare for every $1 earned—in effect, a 100 percent tax. During the next fourteen years, earned income was treated more generously in order to promote work among recipients and raise their overall income. In 1981 the Reagan administration, contending that any employment signified self-sufficiency, persuaded Congress to drastically reduce AFDC benefits for workers. Congress subsequently

Figure 16. Legislative changes in 1981 reduced the number of AFDC recipients with earned income.

1979   1990

Source: U.S. Health and Human Services Department

loosened the 1981 restrictions, but the treatment of earnings remains much more stringent than in 1980. Under current rules, a mother with two children who had been on the welfare rolls for one year and earned $581 monthly would, after deductions, have a net countable income of $391 for the purposes of determining the AFDC payment. In 1980 the net countable income would have been $187, and the mother would have consequently received a much higher AFDC payment. The percentage of AFDC recipients with reported income from earnings dropped from 13 percent in 1979 to 6 percent in 1983, before rising slightly to 8 percent in 1990 (Figure 16).

The combined effect of lower AFDC benefit levels and stricter earnings disregards has made it difficult for workers to combine even low earnings with AFDC benefits. In 1980, a worker with earnings equal to 75 percent of the poverty line qualified for AFDC benefits in forty-two states. By 1992, a worker with earnings at that level qualified for AFDC benefits in only five states.

In 1990, 22 percent of poor households in which the head worked at some point during the year obtained AFDC or general assistance, and in the previous year AFDC benefits had raised 17 percent of working-poor beneficiaries above the poverty threshold. In many cases AFDC assistance may have been received during the out-of-work periods. Cash welfare also had a significant impact by reducing the difference between the average 1989 income of working-poor households and the poverty line (the poverty gap) by 10 percent.

In-Kind Benefits

The major means-tested in-kind benefit programs include food stamps, medical care, and housing assistance. Real spending for these programs has increased dramatically since the mid-1960s, but in 1989 no more than two-fifths of poor families with working household heads received food stamps, the most frequently obtained noncash benefit. A much higher percentage of the nonworking poor received various in-kind assistance. The percentage of the poor who received in-kind assistance stabilized in the 1980s.

Food

The food-stamp program is especially useful to poor workers, because its eligibility standard is set at the poverty threshold and its earnings disregards are lenient. The federal government sets national benefit standards for the program and supplies most of the funds, but state welfare agencies administer it locally. In 1991 the average monthly value of food stamps per person was $64. In 1992 a family of four with a monthly gross income below $1,452 was eligible to receive food stamps, and the maximum monthly benefit was $370. Thirty percent of the household's net income is deducted in determining the value of benefits. In 1992 a poor family of four wholly reliant on a single full-time, year-round minimum-wage worker who received the maximum childcare- and housing-expense deductions was entitled to $336 worth of food stamps monthly. This amount increased the family's income by 46 percent. The income limits are high enough to include most impoverished workers, but a stringent $2,000 liquid asset limit— excluding the value of a residence, a portion of the value of motor vehicles, and other resources—precludes some poor workers from qualifying for food stamps.

In 1991, 22.6 million individuals received food stamps during an average month, at an estimated price tag for the year of $21 billion. The recession pushed the caseload to a historic peak of 25 million in early 1992, almost 5 million more than at the downturn's outset in July 1990. Food stamps are designed to enable a family to maintain what the U.S. Agriculture Department calls a "nutritionally adequate" diet, but this regimen requires sophisticated nutritional planning, adequate refrigerator space, equipment, and low-cost markets—resources frequently unavailable to the poor. Departmental surveys indicate that 90 percent of families with food expenditures identical to food-stamp levels have inadequate diets.

A fifth of households receiving food stamps had at least one worker in 1989, a proportion that has remained almost constant for the past decade and a half. In the mid-1980s between a third and a half of all eligible households did not obtain food stamps, including a large share of eligible nonrecipients who may have been poor workers.[1]

All reasons	100%
Perceived ineligibility, or unaware of program	37
Did not need food stamps	29
Did not want to face bureaucratic hassles	13
Qualms about welfare receipt	10
Welfare officials told them they were ineligible	9
Transportation obstacles	3

In 1990, 39 percent of poor households with a working head obtained an average of $1,680 in food stamps. In the previous year, 8 percent of recipient households would have been lifted above the poverty line if the stamps were counted as cash. Food stamps would also have reduced the poverty gap of poor working households by 9 percent in 1989. In addition, free or subsidized school breakfasts and lunches benefited two-fifths of working-poor households in 1990, and in the prior year another 8 percent obtained food from the supplemental food program for women, infants, and children (WIC), which assists pregnant women, as well as children up to 5 years old.

Health Care

Only half of poor workers are covered by health insurance, which implies potentially dire consequences for their health and a disincentive to work for those who can obtain AFDC. In 1990 poor individuals who worked full-time, year-round were less likely to be covered by health insurance than individuals aged 16 to 64 who did not work at all (54 versus 68 percent). This imbalance is largely due to the Medicaid program, which guarantees coverage to AFDC recipients. Poor workers aged 16 to 64 rarely obtain health coverage through their own employment, and they are more likely to be covered through either Medicaid or another family member's policy.

	Total covered	Total privately covered	Total covered through own job	Total covered through Medicaid
Poor workers	53%	31%	15%	22%
Full-time, year-round	54	44	28	9
Poor nonworkers	68	16	2*	53

*Obtained coverage through a former job.

In addition, 4 percent of working-poor households included someone with Medicare coverage, although this insurance covers only the individual and not other family members.

Recent Medicaid reforms have expanded health insurance coverage for the working poor with children, but these improvements have not outweighed cuts in private insurance and declines in Medicaid coverage since the early 1980s. The decline in employer-provided health insurance since 1979 has been entirely concentrated among the bottom half of earners, as employees making more than $34,000 (1992 dollars) maintained their coverage rates in the succeeding decade.[2] In contrast, the coverage of poor workers with employer- or union-provided health insurance fell from 31 percent in 1979 to 19 percent in 1987. Much of the drop occurred in the first half of the 1980s, but both employer-provided and total private health insurance coverage rates for the working poor have continued to fall in recent years.

After 1967 the expansion of AFDC to some poor workers concomitantly boosted their Medicaid coverage. But the curtailment of AFDC to the working poor in 1981 also denied them Medicaid eligibility. Recent Medicaid amendments have not explicitly targeted the working poor, but required the states to extend coverage to children in poor families not receiving AFDC. The 1990 Omnibus Budget Reconciliation Act requires states to cover all poor children by year 2001. The 1988 Family Support Act provided that individuals who leave the AFDC rolls because of increased earnings may retain Medicaid coverage for as long as one year, although the states may require payment for coverage during the second half of the year. Other reforms have extended coverage to children in near-poor families. Of course, these expansions will not aid poor workers without children. Moreover, rapid inflation of health-care costs has increasingly stretched state resources, prompting efforts to block Medicaid extensions.[3] This inflation is also a significant cause of declining employer-provided health insurance coverage for poor workers.

Shelter

In 1990 only 15 percent of working-poor households lived in publicly owned or subsidized private rental housing. The average recipient obtained nearly $2,400 worth of housing subsidies, which would have lifted one-fifth of beneficiaries above the poverty line if these benefits were counted as cash. The nonworking poor were twice as likely to receive housing aid. Ironically, the federal mortgage interest tax deductions subsidizes the housing costs of nonpoor homeowners more generously than the rental expenses of the poor. Only ten states provide tax breaks to nonelderly, low-income renters.

Information on the shelter expenses of poor workers (two-thirds of whom are renters) is not available, but because they obtain less government housing assistance than the nonworking poor their shelter costs are unquestionably a heavy burden. In 1989 the housing costs of nonelderly households with an annual income between $5,000 and $10,000 accounted for on average 35 percent of income. Moreover, utility, heating fuel, and telephone expenses accounted for another 17 percent of income. Thus the working poor probably spend half of their income for shelter.[4] The U.S. Department of Housing and Urban Development's housing subsidy guidelines recommend that housing expenses should not exceed 30 percent of income.

Largely because the private housing market has failed to increase the nation's stock of low-income housing, the availability of affordable housing for the poor has declined sharply during the past two decades. Applying the guidelines of a 30 percent maximum housing cost to an annual income of $10,000 yields a maximum monthly shelter cost of $250. Adjusted for inflation, the share of units that rented for less than $250 a month has fallen by almost half, from 29 to 16 percent in the past two decades. In 1989 the number of rental units costing less than $250 (including utilities) per month indicated an "affordability" gap for some 4 million households where none existed two decades earlier.[5]

	1970	1989
	(millions)	
Rental units costing $250 monthly	6.8	5.5
Renter households with under $10,000 annual income	6.4	9.6
Affordability gap	−0.4	4.1

Poor workers have benefited little from increases in government housing assistance. Inflation-adjusted outlays for U.S. Housing and Urban Development programs have nearly tripled since 1977, from $6.6 billion to an estimated $18.6 billion in 1992. The percentage of poor renters who receive government housing assistance rose from 23 to 36 percent in the decade after 1979.[6] However, the percentage of working-poor renters who lived in publicly owned or subsidized units barely grew, from 16 percent in 1979 to 19 percent in 1987, while the percentage of nonworking, nonelderly poor renters who obtained housing assistance rose from 30 to 43 percent. By almost eliminating new construction projects, the federal government has abandoned the most direct means of ensuring an adequate supply of affordable housing. To an unknown extent, rental assistance partly subsidizes landlords rather than tenants, and it is consequently not as effective at increasing the supply of low-income apartments. Fraud has also diverted a significant amount of housing funding away from the intended low-income beneficiaries.

Social Insurance

Federal social insurance supports workers when they retire, lose their jobs, or become disabled. In contrast to means-tested programs, assets and other nonearned income are ignored for purposes of determining social insurance benefits. Social insurance program outlays dwarf expenditures for means-tested programs, and they enjoy widespread public support by virtue of their near-universal coverage.

Social Security

Social security is the largest and most acclaimed income support program. It is of particular help to retired low-wage workers. In February 1992, 36.1 million retired workers or their survivors received social security retirement benefits, at a cost of $23.9 billion. The 1983 revision of social security was designed to ensure that the system remains financially sound for the balance of the twentieth century and beyond.

One in three elderly individuals was impoverished in 1960. Primarily because of more generous social security benefits, that proportion fell to less than one in eight by 1990. In 1989 social security and railroad retirement benefits reduced poverty among the elderly by 75 percent. Lenient requirements extend social security benefits to most individuals who were low-wage workers before retirement, and benefit levels are weighted in favor of these workers. The proportion of earnings replaced by social security is much greater for low earners than for high ones, as demonstrated in the case of three hypothetical 1990 retirees.

Lifetime earnings equal to	*Earnings replaced*
45% of average earner	58%
Average earner	43
Maximum taxable social security wage	25

Although few low-income working households receive social security, the program significantly prevents impoverishment by lifting 71 percent of 1989 beneficiaries who would otherwise be poor above the poverty threshold. Only the least well paid social security recipients remain poor, but even these households obtained almost $4,500 worth of benefits in 1990.

Private Pensions

Low-wage workers are dependent on social security benefits in their retirement years either because their employers rarely provide retirement benefits or because the high turnover rate associated with their jobs prevents them from acquiring a vested pension. In the three decades before 1979, the proportion of workers covered by private pensions more than doubled. But subsequently pension coverage has dropped, especially among poor workers. Less than one in six wage and salaried poor workers are covered by private pensions, compared to more than two in five nonpoor employees.[7]

Disability Assistance

Assistance to the disabled is more fragmented than aid for other needy groups. The $28 billion social security disability insurance program is the largest, but it accounts for only about a third of total cash assistance to the disabled. Other major programs that largely, if not exclusively, assist the disabled include workers' compensation, supplemental security income, veterans' benefits, and various programs for government workers. The growing costs of disability insurance since its inception in 1956 and concerns that it encouraged dependency led to 1980 amendments that lowered benefit levels for future beneficiaries, induced recipients to work, and required a review of disability status every three years. Consequently, the caseload leveled off during the 1980s. However, in the early 1990s the number of disabled worker recipients climbed to 3.2 million. The reasons for the upswing are not yet clear, but the recession and more liberal assessments of applicants and current beneficiaries provide a partial explanation. Even before the upturn, more than half of severely disabled working-age individuals received disability insurance, supplemental security income, or both, and an unknown proportion of the remainder obtained assistance from other programs.

The expansion of aid to the disabled has probably contributed to declining labor force participation rates among preretirement men, but the connection is far from unequivocal. Even applicants rejected for disability insurance, who presumably are healthier than beneficiaries, tend to have very limited subsequent work experience. Half of the applicants rejected in 1984 were jobless three years later. Most had not worked at all in the period, and half of those with jobs earned less—usually at least 25 percent less—than they did prior to applying for disability. Some 43 percent of disability insurance recipients are poor.[8]

Unemployment Insurance

Unemployment insurance (UI) is designed to help tide over the unemployed during spells of joblessness and to stimulate the economy during recessions. Eligibility and benefits are based on past earnings and work experience, not on need. Consequently, UI provides some help to the working poor, compared to none for the nonworking poor, although in certain ways the program unfairly treats the working poor relative to better paid employees.

Employers pay UI taxes that cover 97 percent of wage and salary workers. However, eligibility rules often deny benefits to presumably covered poor workers who lose their jobs. Depending upon the state, the unemployed applicant must have earned from $130 to $5,000 in the previous year to receive the minimum benefit. These minimum earnings requirements force low-wage earners, who are the most susceptible to unemployment, to work more hours than high-wage earners in order to qualify for UI. However, if poor workers manage to qualify, the program's benefit formulas usually replace a higher proportion of lost earnings for low-wage employees. State UI benefits typically range between 50 and 70 percent of previous earnings, up to a maximum amount. In 1992 a jobless individual who had worked full-time, year-round at the minimum wage received UI benefits ranging from $77 to $176 weekly, depending upon the state.

The system's financing structure is extremely regressive, which also tends to hurt low-wage workers. In 1992 the federal taxable wage base was $7,000, less than 40 percent of average earnings; in 1940 the tax base was 90 percent of the average. Although employers pay the UI tax, economists generally assume that much of the tax is passed on to workers in the form of lower wages.

Tighter eligibility rules, resulting from federal and state UI restrictions in the early 1980s, have contributed to a drastic reduction in the scope of unemployment benefits. Prior to the recent recession, only a third of the unemployed received benefits—a record low since the end of World War II. Poor workers have been hit hardest by the system's declining protection. In the mid-1980s less than a fifth of unemployed workers who had earned less than $7,000 annually received UI, compared to half of those who had earned more than $10,000. Following past recessionary patterns, the percentage of unemployed who received UI rose to 42 percent during 1991.[9] The increase was primarily due to a change in the composition of the unemployed as a result of the recession. In late 1991 and twice in 1992 Congress extended temporary payments to beneficiaries whose regular coverage had expired, but workers ineligible to receive benefits were denied assistance. Thus poor workers who became jobless benefited little from the extension.

Although few poor workers who become jobless receive UI, the program often prevents poverty among recipients facing lengthy unemployment. Even with UI, 20 percent of those who obtained benefits for more than three months became impoverished for at least one month while jobless, but their poverty rate would have risen to 46 percent without UI.[10]

How Much Assistance?

Although government programs provide more help to the non-working than the working poor, the latter group benefits substantially from government aid. Government cash aid and food stamps lifted 30 percent of workers out of poverty who otherwise would have been poor in 1990, compared to 38 percent in 1979 (Table 9). The transfers also reduced the poverty gap by slightly more than

Table 9. Federal assistance ameliorates poverty among workers (1990)

| | | Worker poverty gap | |
	Worker poverty rate (aged 20 to 64)	Families (aged 15 to 64)	Unrelated individuals (aged 20 to 64)
Income			
Official definition minus government cash transfers	8.1%	$5,372	$3,043
Official definition	6.4	4,593	2,857
Including noncash benefits and taxes	5.6	3,916	2,546

Source: U.S. Census Bureau

Figure 17. The antipoverty effectiveness of government cash and food stamp benefits for poor workers declined during the 1980s.

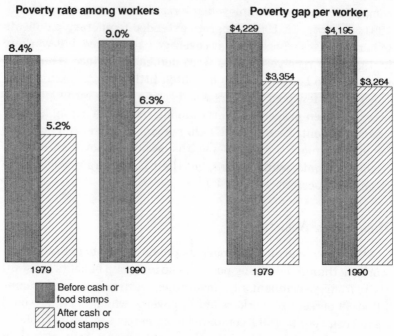

Source: Current Population Survey tabulations by Andrew Sum, Northeastern University

a fifth (Figure 17). Because some survey respondents under-report their receipt of government benefits, official statistics understate the impact of government assistance in reducing poverty for both the working and the nonworking poor. In addition, Census Bureau surveys do not explicitly measure the anti-poverty impact of some important benefits, such as the minimum wage and education or training.

Governmental and employer-provided health insurance further lighten the burden of poor workers. Including the effects of taxes, in 1990 government in-kind benefits reduced the poverty gap of working families by 15 percent and that of unrelated individuals by 11 percent.[11]

The earned income tax credit, food stamps, AFDC, and social

security provide the most help to the working poor. Social security benefits lift most recipient working households above the poverty threshold. Conversely, the earned income tax credit and food stamps are worth much less, but, because a much larger share of poor working households obtain them, these programs significantly reduce the overall poverty gap. AFDC is important not only because some of the poor simultaneously work and receive welfare but also because some poor workers receive AFDC during jobless spells. Altogether, social insurance programs lift nearly three-fifths of recipient working households above the poverty line (Table 10).

Nonworking households receive twice the estimated value of benefits per household obtained by poor working households; the former receive $1 in means-tested benefits for every $1 of private household income (Figure 18). Some of this imbalance is defensible because of the larger share of nonworking poor individuals who cannot work due to health problems, and because nonworkers are more destitute. Moreover, even after factoring in government benefits and taxes, poor nonworkers remain more destitute than poor workers (Table 11).

State, local, and federal governments spend substantial sums not only on the foregoing programs but also on preparation for work through the educational system. Those who fail or are failed by this system are more likely to receive in-kind or income help than assistance that promotes economic self-sufficiency. Social insurance, in-kind benefits, and cash welfare expenditures dwarf outlays for second-chance education and training programs. The former are not an efficient use of government funds, except when individuals are incapable of work. In contrast to training and education, most income-support costs are not offset by productivity increases or declines in other areas of government spending. There are exceptions to this generalization. For example, the prevention of malnutrition among children by governmental food assistance not only helps children become productive citizens but also tends to reduce subsequent medical costs. Although promoting economic self-sufficiency is the best long-term approach to the problems of the working poor, if employment fails to bring individuals and their families out of poverty, income-support programs provide necessary assistance to them.

Table 10. The earned income tax credit, food stamps, social security, and AFDC most benefit working-poor households (1989)

Program	Benefit as a percentage of nontransfer income	Percentage of		
		Poor workers removed from poverty	Beneficiaries removed from poverty	Reduction in poverty gap
Social insurance[a]	36%	16%	58%	18%
Social security	24	13	71	14
Unemployment insurance	3	2	25	3
Medicare	7	6	42	5
Means-tested assistance[b]	30	22	34	34
AFDC or general assistance	6	3	17	10
Earned income tax credit	5	5	11	7
Food stamps	7	2	8	9
Public/subsidized housing	4	2	19	5
Medicaid	4	5	16	6

Source: U.S. Census Bureau, unpublished data

[a]Includes listed programs, as well as workers' compensation and black-lung benefits. Poverty is defined as income exclusive of government cash benefits.

[b]Includes listed programs, as well as veterans benefits, subsidized school lunches, and energy assistance. The first column uses the official poverty definition. The remaining three columns define poverty on the basis of the official definition minus means-tested cash transfers.

Figure 18. Government means-tested benefits are far more generous to nonworking than to working poor households (1989).

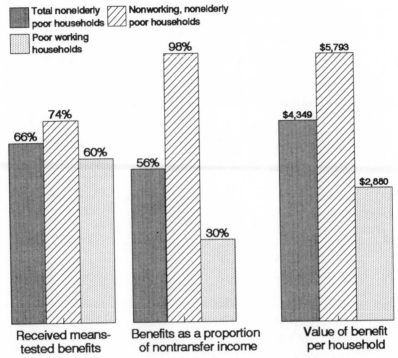

Source: U.S. Census Bureau, unpublished data based on official poverty definition

Work and Welfare

Employment policy for the poor should have two aims. One is to ensure that work time and earnings are sufficient to keep workers from impoverishment. The other is to promote work by the able-bodied, nonworking poor, in order to enhance their economic prospects and prevent welfare dependency. The former goal has received much less attention than the latter, because of widespread resentment of cash subsidies for able-bodied, nonworking individuals.

The Aid to Families with Dependent Children program has remained controversial since its inception. The growth of AFDC was largely the product of several unforeseen historical develop-

Table 11. Government benefit and tax policies significantly reduce the poverty gap differential between the nonworking and working poor (1990)

	Poverty gap	
	Before transfers and taxes	After transfers and taxes
Families (members aged 15 to 64)		
Did not work	$9,651	$4,659
Worked	5,372	3,916
Ratio of nonworkers to workers	180%	119%
Unrelated individuals (aged 20 to 64)		
Did not work	6,118	3,970
Worked	3,043	2,546
Ratio of nonworkers to workers	201%	156%

Source: U.S. Census Bureau

ments, and it is highly unlikely that if AFDC did not exist today, the federal government would enact the current program. Society viewed the widowed mothers who were the original beneficiaries as victims impoverished through no fault of their own and therefore deserving of assistance. Contemporary mores held that the proper role of these women was child-rearing rather than paid work. But by the 1960s the characteristics of both society and welfare mothers had begun to change radically. First, as mothers of every socioeconomic status entered the labor market en masse, the rationale for supporting jobless AFDC mothers weakened. Second, divorce and out-of-wedlock births, rather than widowhood, became the primary causes of eligibility, and these conditions have engendered far less sympathy among taxpayers, many of whom regarded never-married mothers as especially "undeserving." The sharp rise in the AFDC caseload further eroded public support for the program.[12]

Critics of AFDC have argued, with some justification, that the program inevitably discourages the work ethic. In fact, AFDC contains stronger work disincentives than other social programs because it assists many able-bodied individuals. Eligibility is not contingent upon an established work history, as required by social insurance programs, except for the small AFDC unemployed parent component. AFDC assists most poor single mothers who do not work, and benefits may be provided for many years. In 1989, 2.8 million poor individuals aged 16 to 64 living in single-parent families claimed that they had no earnings. In the same year, there were more than 2 million nonworking women on AFDC.

The evidence suggests that AFDC discourages work, but ascertaining the precise extent is difficult if not impossible. Providing jobs to able-bodied recipients in return for assistance would alleviate the public's perception that AFDC encourages malingering and would help the recipients achieve self-sufficiency. It would likely raise the income as well as the self-esteem of recipients, and the public would almost certainly endorse higher payments to workers than to nonworkers. A combination of education, training, and subsidized jobs would enhance the upward mobility of AFDC recipients. The federal government has taken halting steps in this direction, first in the late 1960s and again two decades later, but the cost of such efforts has proved a major roadblock.

During the program's first quarter of a century, the federal government actively discouraged the states from requiring individuals to perform work in return for AFDC. However, the creation in 1961 of the AFDC unemployed parent program negated claims that recipients should not or could not work, prompting the federal government a year later to permit states to operate work/welfare projects. Few states did so, and subsequent employment requirements had little impact until the federal government boosted funding of these programs during the 1970s. By 1980, employment and training programs spent nearly $3 billion (1992 dollars) to assist AFDC recipients through education, training, and subsidized employment:

	Estimated outlays (1980) (millions)
Total	$2,867
Comprehensive Employment and Training Act	2,192
Public service employment	1,099
Training	762
Youth employment and training program	331
Work Incentive Program	675

This amount was sufficient to assist only a minority of recipients, but subsequent cuts reduced outlays by three-fourths before enactment of the 1988 Family Support Act.

Food-Stamp Employment Program

The 1985 Food Security Act required the states to establish an employment program for food-stamp recipients. The federal government has guaranteed the states $75 million annually and has pledged to match additional state spending on a one-to-one basis. Total federal/state employment outlays for food-stamp recipients have been about $225 million annually. The available funding permitted an average of only about $135 per participant in 1988.

Given the minuscule funding, a federally funded evaluation of the program found that it had no impact in raising participants' employment or earnings, and that the savings in food-stamp outlays were less than the employment program's costs. With so little money, the employment program provided little more than brief job search assistance to enrollees.[13] These findings suggest that there is little justification for continuing a separate employment program for food-stamp recipients. Instead, Congress should consider merging the program with JTPA.

JOBS

The Job Opportunities and Basic Skills (JOBS) program, part of the 1988 Family Support Act, has revived work-related assistance to welfare recipients. The program's most important changes include higher federal funding and new participation rate requirements. However, the availability of federal funds is contingent upon the states meeting financial matching requirements instituted for the first time. The recession that began in mid-1990 undoubtedly impaired the implementation of JOBS. AFDC caseloads swelled by almost 3 million people, while states were trying to raise money to fully fund JOBS. Even if the states spend enough to avail themselves of all federal matching JOBS funds, however, the overall work/welfare investment would fall short of the levels attained in 1980.

Fiscal year	Federal matching funds	Federal funds obligated by states
1989	$600	$48
1990	800	383
1991	1,000	599

JOBS requires the states to progressively increase the participation of AFDC recipients in the program, reaching 20 percent by 1995 for single-parent families and 75 percent by 1997 for two-parent families. The law also tightened exemptions, requiring participation by parents whose youngest child is at least 3 years old, and the states may require parents with 1- or 2-year-olds to enroll. Only seven states have done so, presumably because mothers of toddlers are less likely to successfully complete training or education courses. Parents who refuse to enroll will lose their personal welfare payment, although payment for the children will continue.

The new law allows states to offer a variety of education, training, and work experience programs. To remove obstacles to successful enrollment in and completion of a training or education program, the federal government expanded childcare assistance. Families that attain self-support retain entitlement for childcare and health-care services for as long as one year. Program administrators must give priority to long-term welfare recipients and to young parents with little education or work experience.

An assessment of JOBS is necessarily tentative at this point because the law established a lengthy implementation period, the U.S. Health and Human Services Department has perfunctorily monitored the program, and the recession undoubtedly impaired operations. The law required the states to operate JOBS statewide by October 1992. The federal government has collected little information on JOBS, and much of what has been gathered is of limited value. The department has not required the states to collect information on whether participants completed their programs, exhibited gains in knowledge or skills, or found jobs. Consequently, the federal government and program administrators are incapable of spotting emerging problems, let alone correcting them. It is doubtful whether JOBS will significantly diminish public criti-

Table 12. JOBS participants enrolled in education or training programs (first quarter of 1991)

	Enrollment
Total	343,500
Distribution	115.0%[a]
Education/training	*76.9*
Secondary education	32.8
Postsecondary education	12.0
Classroom job training	19.0
Self-initiated education/training	13.1
Job search/job readiness	*25.7*
Job search	18.5
Job readiness	7.2
Subsidized work	*5.0*
On-the-job training	1.2
Work supplementation	.2
Work experience	3.6
Other	*7.4*

Source: JOBS administrative data, U.S. Health and Human Services Department
[a]Some participants received multiple forms of assistance.

cism of AFDC. Unless present participation targets are raised, the vast majority of able-bodied recipients will be left out of the program.

The ideological contest between advocates who endorsed workfare (work in return for welfare) and those who favored education and training for AFDC recipients has so far been won by the latter group. The law itself clearly favors education and training, which are mandatory, as opposed to optional subsidized employment programs used sparingly by the states. Bearing in mind that some double-counting occurs in the data collection system, approximately three-fourths of JOBS participants enroll in education or training programs, versus only about 5 percent in some form of subsidized work. About half of the total enroll in education courses, mostly at the high school level (Table 12).

Insufficient public transportation has impeded JOBS to some extent. Virtually all states report inadequate public transportation to JOBS sites, especially in rural areas.[14] Given the dire poverty of AFDC families and the program's strict eligibility rules concerning cars, adequate public transportation is critically important. The Family Support Act requires the states to pay for transportation and other work-related support services to enable an individual's participation in JOBS.

Most states also report that childcare needs for recipients exceed supply, especially for preschoolers. The law mandates that JOBS participants be provided with childcare if they require it in order to enroll. The fact that the federal government did not place a cap on total childcare expenditures—in contrast to the limits on services directly related to work—is a telling indication of the emphasis given to this need. In the first three months of 1991, a monthly average of 185,000 children obtained AFDC-subsidized childcare, and total fiscal 1991 AFDC childcare outlays were $308 million. Additional JOBS enrollees undoubtedly receive childcare assistance from other public childcare programs, although the number is unknown.

The perception that virtually all AFDC mothers require subsidized childcare in order to participate in work/welfare programs is erroneous. Surveys of JOBS' predecessor, the work incentive program, indicated that half of all participants—a third of whom had children younger than age 6—did not need childcare assistance at the time of the survey. Even in cases where the mothers needed childcare, a third of the children were looked after by relatives. JOBS patterns reinforce this finding because, during the first three months of 1991, no more than a third of average monthly participants obtained AFDC-subsidized childcare.

In mid-1992 preliminary results were available for only one program similar to JOBS, California's Greater Avenues for Independence (GAIN) program, which was enacted in 1985. Early results from six of the state's fifty-eight counties indicate small increases in earnings and lower welfare payments one year after enrollment, compared to a control group that did not enroll in GAIN.[15]

Participants compared to controls	AFDC, single parents	AFDC, unemployed parents
Annual earnings gains	$271	$375
percentage	17%	15%
Annual AFDC savings	$281	$420
percentage	5%	6%

Prospects for Success

Although most adult AFDC recipients are able-bodied, they have a slim chance of securing sustained employment that pays wages above the poverty level. Half never finished high school, few have recent work experience and a substantial number have never worked, and almost all are single parents. The U.S. Education Department's 1982 literacy test found that more than one-fourth of AFDC and food-stamp recipients aged 20 to 39 were functionally illiterate. Conclusive evidence is lacking, but lengthy recipiency probably makes individuals progressively less employable, both in their own minds due to discouragement and certainly in the eyes of prospective employers.

To promote upward mobility, acquisition of further education, skills, and job experience is essential. Intensive education and/or occupational training and subsidized employment are the two most potentially useful employment-related measures. Although the statutory language of the Family Support Act emphasizes education, U.S. Health and Human Services Department regulations discourage it. The present rule requiring at least twenty hours of class attendance weekly is unreasonable for a young mother raising children.[16] If the rule is continued, administrators should be allowed to credit a specific amount of homework performed to meet the twenty-hour requirement.

Education and occupational training pay off for other Americans, and there is no reason why they should not benefit most AFDC recipients. But the large number of AFDC recipients who are high school dropouts or functional illiterates and possess unquestionably negative attitudes toward school will impede further education. Combining occupational training with education, as in the Job Corps, may prove the most effective technique.

Public-service employment would meet a variety of needs in a work/welfare effort. It would endorse the principle that individuals have obligations in return for benefits, the absence of which has made AFDC enduringly unpopular with the public. Recipients themselves and their children would benefit from this reform, for the public would be more willing to pay higher wages to AFDC adults than the meager benefits available currently. Graduates of education or training programs unable to find private-sector jobs would be able to garner work experience that should facilitate subsequent private-sector employment. Subsidized jobs have enhanced the earnings of even long-term AFDC recipients. The post-program earnings record of public-service employees during the 1970s stacked up well against both classroom and on-the-job occupational training. More intensive employment-related assistance is potentially promising but expensive, even though AFDC benefits would offset about a third of the costs of public-service employment.

General Assistance

State and local general assistance programs provide cash and health coverage to some individuals ineligible for AFDC or Supplemental Security Income. These programs vary widely in scope, but are generally quite limited, and eight states do not offer general assistance. Most recipients are single adults, and the states have increasingly restricted help to the able-bodied by limiting the duration of recipiency or excluding them from the programs altogether.[17] Because the programs are not federally funded, the states were free to implement the workfare requirements long prohibited in AFDC. Consequently some general assistance programs have mandated workfare for decades. Recipients are eligible for food stamps.

Information on general assistance is incomplete, but the available reports indicate that caseloads increased after 1989 by 200,000 to 1.1 million in 1991. The states spent an estimated $3.2 billion in 1990 for cash aid. Six states—New York, Pennsylvania, Ohio, Michigan, California, and Illinois—accounted for four-fifths of the national caseload, with nearly one-quarter in New York alone.

Benefits are not generous, but in three of the six states the maximum payment approximated the AFDC level. In 1989 the median maximum payment slightly exceeded $200 monthly, ranging from $148 in Ohio (later cut to $100) to $334 in New York. In all but one of these states the maximum inflation-adjusted payment has fallen since 1982. All six states also provide health coverage.

Until recently all six states provided benefits without time limits to income-eligible able-bodied individuals, who constituted the largest share of their caseloads, but during the recession Michigan eliminated all assistance to employable individuals, and Illinois and Ohio instituted time limits. None of the states operated separate general assistance work programs, but all required recipients to enroll in AFDC work programs, which all included workfare as well as education and training components. How strictly the participation requirements were enforced, and what kinds of work-related assistance predominated, is unknown.[18]

Work Incentives and Welfare Reform

Minimizing out-of-wedlock births, drug use, and other obstacles to self-sufficiency are as important as work/welfare efforts in preventing or alleviating poverty among able-bodied AFDC adult recipients or potential recipients. Therefore, stressing rectitude is crucial, and the welfare system should offer adequate incentives to current and potential AFDC recipients to make work and self-sufficiency more rewarding than dependency.

The governmental pressure exerted in recent years to identify absent parents and secure child support from them should be intensified, but these efforts will be limited by the fact that poor women tend to become involved with poor men. Therefore, work/welfare programs should also target absent fathers who are jobless or have limited earnings. Fathers who do not bear the responsibilities of child-rearing should be assisted in assuming them. The U.S. Health and Human Services Department is mounting a demonstration project to include noncustodial, unemployed parents in JOBS.

The concern with the work disincentives inherent in the welfare system is justified. Many recipients depend on AFDC as a temporary means of support, but taxpayers frequently resent paying taxes to support those who are able to work but make no effort to do so. The welfare system should help individuals who cannot work, who look for work but are unsuccessful in obtaining it, and who work but remain in poverty. These individuals find it difficult to make ends meet and deserve public support, including wage supplements to help them escape poverty.

The current system provides a measure of economic security to many, but falls short in helping poor workers and their families fulfill their basic needs. The debate over work disincentives should not ignore the working poor, because this neglect is itself a powerful work disincentive and a cause of deprivation.

8. Looking Down the Road

As this volume goes to press in late 1992, the nation is in the midst of a political campaign to select its next leaders. Barring unforeseen catastrophes, U.S. domestic problems are likely to receive much greater attention in the years ahead, but the immediate direction of future policy is heavily dependent upon the upcoming election results, as well as the implementation of the promises made by the victorious candidate.

Meanwhile, the problems of the working poor persist and have been aggravated in important respects. After the longest peacetime recovery since World War II, poverty rates among workers in 1989 remained above the low point in 1979, and, of course, poor workers lost ground during the 1990–91 recession. Growing inequality in earnings has hit poor workers hardest, international competition continues to depress wages, pockets of economic dislocation abound, and millions of workers lack basic skills. Recent legislative enactments indicate progress but will raise relatively few workers out of poverty, and the overall effort remains below the level of governmental assistance in the 1970s.

Free market enthusiasts recommend letting the market take its course, arguing that government intervention—particularly at the federal level—will only exacerbate existing problems. The Bush administration has taken a less purist stance, while liberals tend to favor a reaffirmation of the role of government in aiding the poor. They advocate reducing unemployment through expansionary macroeconomic policy; increasing the minimum wage; expanding education, employment, and training programs; and supplementing the income of poor workers through the welfare and tax systems.

During the past decade the attitudes of leaders and other individuals with various political beliefs have converged somewhat on issues relevant to poor workers. Persistent poverty even after a lengthy economic recovery has convinced many conservatives that the government must play an active role in any serious antipoverty effort. Poverty preceded the welfare state, and government programs have ameliorated impoverishment, not caused it. Liberals have become more attuned to the need to promote the work ethic and to avoid the undesirable effects that can result when government programs sustain able-bodied individuals regardless of their behavior.

This new accommodation has produced bipartisan expansions of the earned income tax credit, programs to facilitate self-sufficiency for welfare recipients, childcare, and literacy assistance. However, the government has yet to sufficiently focus on the importance of promoting work in designing policies and programs.

For example, a pressing need of poor workers—who are usually jobless part of the year and often work part-time during other months—is additional work time. In 1981 the federal government abandoned the last major jobs program for the poor. Poor working-age individuals who do not work at all are more likely to possess health insurance than low-wage full-time, year-round workers.

The earned income tax credit promotes work, but by assisting only parents it ignores the importance of work incentives for the nearly half of poor workers who are childless. Workers who display rectitude by postponing child-rearing until they can command sufficient earnings to keep their family out of poverty also deserve consideration. Similarly, the minimum wage attempts to ensure a minimally decent living standards for workers, but in the 1980s the government ignored the fact that inflation inexorably eroded its value. The federal government has acknowledged the corrosive power of inflation by automatically adjusting social security benefits and taxes for price changes. Similar treatment of the minimum wage is long overdue.

In reforming established programs and designing new efforts, policymakers should explicitly perform an impact assessment: Does this program encourage and reward work effort, or do able-bodied individuals who demonstrate no inclination to work receive the same benefits as those who work long hours? Many antipoverty programs fail this test. For example, changes in the AFDC program in the early 1980s made it more difficult for welfare recipients to earn their way out of poverty.

The Need for Federal Intervention

Even if the pace of economic growth is accelerated, in the absence of increased federal intervention the convergence of work and poverty will continue to mar the lives of millions of individuals and their families. Sustained economic growth will benefit the working poor in some areas, but rural and inner-city economies may not benefit even if nearby areas prosper. The mismatch between available jobs and the skill levels of the unemployed or underemployed also needs to be addressed. Millions of Americans who lack basic skills will not find higher-paying jobs even in an expanding national economy.

In mid-1992, 9.5 million Americans remained unemployed, 6.1 million workers were employed part-time because they could not find full-time work, and 1.1 million individuals became discouraged and gave up looking for jobs. Deep recession conditions, with unemployment exceeding 7 percent, prevailed in 9 of the 10 most populated states. Even in states with below-average unemployment rates, there were metropolitan areas with seriously troubled economies. In early 1992, nearly a quarter of the 255 metropolitan areas for which information was available experienced unemployment rates of 8.5 percent or more. Some areas in Texas and Massachusetts had joblessness exceeding 15 percent. A reduction in the national unemployment rate will, at best, only partially ameliorate these local labor market problems.

Ongoing economic trends do not bode well for the working poor. In addition to the high unemployment rate, income distribution is becoming more skewed in favor of the affluent. Although trade deficits have declined, they continue to contribute to loose labor markets, causing a loss of jobs and dampening wage growth. The budget deficit has hindered an activist federal role.

Despite these problems, government policy has made important strides in helping poor workers, even if they are not always the explicit beneficiaries of new or expanded programs. However, these improvements have occurred against a background of increasing disadvantages that poor workers face in the private economy. Absent remedial action by the private sector, more forceful government action is needed just to keep poor workers from falling further behind. Destitution and its accompanying crime, health, and other social problems will not go away in the absence of government intervention. Failure to address poverty problems vigorously and promptly will only increase the burden on future generations.

The Task Ahead

Given the uncertain turn of economic and political developments, overly specific recommendations may be quickly superseded by unforeseen events. Therefore, this closing chapter outlines the most pressing needs of poor workers and examines how best to confront and alleviate the problems they face. This may require augmenting the financing of a current well-run program or adapting it to aid the working poor. In other instances, a program may be addressed to a worthy goal, but operate so inefficiently in practice that either major reforms or an entirely new approach are necessary. Finally, present policies virtually ignore certain critical needs of poor workers. The recommendations made here could not be enacted and implemented within a single year, but are achievable within the next five to ten years.

Poor workers have been buffeted by major economic and social changes, but decisions about societal responses to these forces cannot be reached with only the working poor in mind. National trade and immigration policies must strike a balance between complex and sometimes conflicting objectives. Trade policy should focus on obtaining access for U.S. exports to foreign markets, weighing the costs of protectionism to the national and international economy against the need to limit job losses due to rising imports. Immigration policy should balance the nation's traditional open door to the "tired, poor, huddled masses" with their impact on wages of U.S. citizens. These issues are of prime importance, but their resolution is beyond the scope of this book.

Our recommendations concentrate on national approaches to

the problems of work and poverty. The idea that states and localities can replace federal antipoverty efforts has been grossly oversold by some, and neither the experience of the past decade nor common sense holds out much promise for substantially ameliorating poverty without federal leadership. Despite much rhetoric, the states did little to compensate for the loss of leadership and funding resulting from the retrenchments during the first term of the Reagan administration. State and local antipoverty expenditures have remained a relatively small and constant share of total antipoverty spending since the early 1980s. Moreover, some states have lobbied to overturn recent federal government mandates requiring additional state expenditures for work/welfare and health-care programs. In addition, state budget deficits in the early 1990s led to cuts in programs that aid the poor.

When states enact social legislation, they find it difficult to achieve more than modest results because of competition from states that fail to enact similar legislation. For example, businesses may relocate to another state if required to provide health insurance or a substantially higher minimum wage. Similarly, states that levy higher taxes in order to fund a comprehensive system of aid to the poor may find their revenue base shrinking as more affluent residents more elsewhere and fewer individuals chose to move into their state.

Of course, the states can and should more actively combat poverty, particularly when the federal government fails to forge ahead. Some states have instituted welfare-to-work programs, enacted state-earned income tax credits, raised their state minimum wages above the federal benchmark, or expanded Medicaid. However, the poverty problem is primarily national in scope, and states or localities acting independently are likely to alleviate impoverishment only marginally.

Some responses to the problems of the working poor would not require additional deficit spending. Whenever feasible, the federal government should use its regulatory authority to ensure that poor workers get a fair deal in the private labor market. A minimum wage that provides a decent standard of living is the most important example. Prevention of employment discrimination is another. In part because of federal tax policy, many firms have provided health insurance and pension coverage in lieu of additional cash compensation. Such tax breaks are less important to low-wage workers. Because most poor workers have been excluded from the fringe benefits enjoyed by the average worker, the federal government should rectify this inequity.

Helping Themselves

In the struggle to make ends meet, individuals themselves are the first line of defense. Government assistance is of little avail unless the poor demonstrate initiative and rectitude. The erosion of the traditional family structure has significantly increased poverty among workers in recent decades. The poverty rate for workers aged 16 to 64 was identical in 1969 and 1989, although the poverty rate declined for each major household type. If the distribution of workers' household structure in 1989 had been the same as two decades earlier, the poverty rate among workers would have been 5.2 rather than 6.4 percent.

Household structure and size can be as important as economic conditions and government assistance in determining poverty. Government policy and economic conditions can and do influence household structure and size, but the ultimate decisions rest with individuals. The same is true of the behavioral choices related to school attendance and learning, crime, and drug abuse. The proper role of government is to reinforce the principles of rectitude, by constructing policies and programs that discourage undesirable behavior and provide incentives that convince the disadvantaged that appropriate personal conduct will pay off.[1]

Divorce is the primary cause of single-parent families. Divorce is, of course, not always a matter of choice, but its occurrence and impact can be reduced if individuals avoid hasty marriages and becoming parents at too young an age; divorce rates are much higher among the young. Government policy should concentrate on helping children, the most important victims of divorce. Mothers, who usually obtain custody, often do not command sufficient earnings to keep their families from impoverishment. The 1988 Family Support Act requires states to establish guidelines for child-support payments. By 1994 such payments will be automatically deducted from the wages of absent parents, guaranteeing single parents a right to a share of them. This reform should reduce poverty among single parents who are workers, but the implementation of past child-support reforms has fallen far short of their promise, and therefore careful monitoring and additional measures may prove necessary. The persistent problem of obtaining child support from jobless absent parents can be addressed by offering the parent a publicly subsidized job. This solution is superior to a jail term, and parents as well as children would benefit.

The same child-support measures should apply in the case of never-married parents, although in this instance the prevention of births through birth control or abstinence is more advisable as well as practical. Teenage out-of-wedlock births often sentence the family to lengthy destitution, and parenthood at such an early age often impedes the pursuit of education, which would permit escape from poverty. However, the vast majority of out-of-wedlock births are to women older than high school age. Prevention of unwanted children is a very effective antipoverty measure whether the parents are married or not. Federal programs providing birth-control instruction, devices, and supplies began a quarter of a century ago. These programs should be expanded, with services and supplies offered at low cost or for free for those who cannot afford them, a policy pursued in other industrialized nations.

Increasing Work Time

Despite a rhetorical adherence to the work ethic, government policy devotes far more resources to transfers for the employable poor than to helping them earn a living. For the able-bodied, government aid should be tied much more closely to work than is the case presently. Cash benefits have never been generous, and their value has eroded significantly over time. However, because the compensation from low-wage jobs has also declined, total AFDC and in-kind benefits too often compare favorably with the rewards available from work, especially for larger families. For example, the fact that full-time, year-round poor workers are less likely to have health insurance than the nonworking poor demonstrates a perverse ordering of government priorities that discourage work. For the able-bodied, AFDC should be transformed from cash assistance to the provision of a job, and health insurance should be extended to the working poor.

Additional paid work is a pressing need for poor workers. Family responsibilities are the most common reason why some individuals are out of the labor force for part of the year. Although important strides have been made in the past few years, much remains to be done to ensure access to affordable childcare. Care for the children of poor workers should be incorporated into a national program to provide childcare for all working parents. The United States exhibits one of the highest female labor-force participation rates in the world, yet stands virtually alone among industrialized countries in the lack of comprehensive childcare policy. Greater reliance on school-based care is the most practical, economical, and educational approach to the problem. Such a program could be doubly beneficial, by providing job opportunities for poor parents.

Market deficiencies explain why many poor workers cannot find full-time work, or any work at all during part of the year. A more effective employment service could cut down on idle spells between jobs and help involuntary part-time workers secure full-time work, but even in a smoothly functioning labor market insufficient job opportunities exist. Government job creation is necessary to fill this gap. Whatever the deficiencies of jobs programs in the past, private-sector solutions such as job subsidies and enterprise zones are inherently subject to abuse and cannot meet the need.[2]

Job creation programs are an extremely versatile means to simultaneously address a variety of unmet needs. Publicly subsidized jobs directly increase paid work time for underemployed poor workers as well as the nonworking poor, and they provide critically needed services. Workers who possess limited skills can fulfill many community needs, including childcare, long-term care for the elderly, teachers' aides, and law-enforcement aides in order to free more police for street duty. Through adjunct classroom or on-the-job training, job holders can be taught skills or trades to facilitate upward mobility. Making jobs available to welfare recipients would not only reinforce the work ethic but also result in increased income for participants and an eventual reduction in public expenditures. The problems of job programs in the past justify improving, not abjuring, future efforts. A recent opinion poll indicated that 71 percent of respondents favored replacing welfare with guaranteed public jobs.[3]

Minimizing job discrimination on the basis of race, ethnicity, religion, gender, and disability would substantially help poor workers, with minimal government spending. With the enactment of the Americans with Disabilities Act, the laws provide sufficient authority to the government to combat discrimination if the will is present. Progress in reducing discrimination has been mixed, with blacks continuing to suffer the most employment bias. Following increasingly vigorous antidiscriminatory policies, the Reagan and Bush administrations (joined more recently by the Supreme Court) drastically scaled back the interpretation and enforcement of laws and policies.

Affirmative action has been enduringly controversial and is now rejected by broad sectors of the public. There is a pressing need to find new tactics to augment current antidiscrimination laws in order to ameliorate a demonstrable wrong. The use of "testers," which in the area of housing discrimination has a proven record and has been endorsed by Congress, should be applied to employment discrimination. This approach should command public support, and, if vigorously implemented, it will deter a significant amount of discrimination.

Boosting Earnings

Low-wage workers have lost ground in the past two decades. Adverse trends in wages as well as benefits necessitate an increasingly vigorous federal role to help low-wage workers from falling further behind. But the federal government has done far too little.

Restoring the minimum wage to the level that existed in the 1960s and 1970s, as well as indexing it to inflation or wage growth, would revive its value. Raising the minimum wage to the poverty line for a three-person family would necessitate slightly more than a $1 increase, to $5.40 (1992 dollars) per hour. Three of four individuals polled in June 1992 favored an increase in the minimum wage to make work more attractive.[4] The increase should be phased in to avoid labor-market problems. Although some job loss would result, the proposed increase is certainly manageable because the minimum wage exceeded this level in the 1960s and 1970s with no discernible problems, even though teenagers and young adults then constituted a larger share of the work force. In addition, the federal government should extend minimum-wage protections and carefully review all present exemptions. Another problem is that significant numbers of salaried employees obtain less than the minimum wage for the number of hours worked. This issue merits a detailed investigation, because it apparently constitutes a hole in the safety net. Finally, Congress should raise the penalties for willful violations of the minimum wage, as well as ensure that the U.S. Labor Department has the personnel to enforce the statute.

The earned income tax credit should be expanded and adjusted for family size. The credit should counteract the payroll taxes paid by poor workers and provide extra income to some. Government standards should also ensure that poor workers obtain important fringe benefits such as health insurance and pension coverage, both of which have become increasingly unavailable to poor workers in the past decade.

Alleviating Skill Deficiencies

The educational inadequacies of poor workers stem from deficiencies in the schools. These problems are well known, but the nation has yet to seriously confront them. The immediate rewards of educational achievement are often slim because many employers are unwilling to hire youth fresh out of school for career-track positions. Consequently many poor youngsters with limited horizons perceive educational effort (sometimes including graduation) as marginal to their careers. National education standards are necessary for practical, legal, and equity considerations. An overwhelming majority of adults now support national tests and curricula. Students polled supported the idea of high school graduation tests, including half who had failed such tests and a higher proportion of minority than white students.

National tests and standards will require careful monitoring, as well as supplementary help to students likely to fail, including the poor. If the standards are set at adequate levels, many students now automatically promoted will likely fail, which may raise dropout rates. In the absence of extra help, students at risk may become the victims rather than the beneficiaries of reform.[5]

Adult education and training efforts are relatively recent additions to the antipoverty arsenal. These programs have been severely underfunded, and the government has often neglected or misdirected its efforts to improve them. The prevalent practice of spreading the minimal resources thinly may be a penny-wise, pound-foolish strategy. Raising the skills of individuals and altering their behavior are considerably more difficult than dispensing cash or providing in-kind assistance, but the efforts should reap greater benefits in the long run.

Financing Reforms

All the recommendations are designed to encourage and enable self-sufficiency, which in the long run should be less costly than supporting idleness. However, in the short-term many of the reforms will require additional spending, and the length of the payoff is unknown because of inherent uncertainties in the economy and in the success of the programs. Three decades of antipoverty policy have demonstrated that promises of immediate social returns are very rarely fulfilled. The suggested reordering of priorities, however, is likely to prove popular with the public even if their implementation results in added outlays. Americans are more willing to expend resources to promote the self-sufficiency of individuals who are working to better their economic prospects than to provide minimal benefits to the able-bodied indolent.

Because of the demise of the Cold War, there exists a unique opportunity to reinvest resources in order to alleviate pressing domestic problems. The nation deserves a more generous peace dividend than the present administration and Congress have been willing to offer. Various agricultural subsidies should also be pruned, although these cutbacks would generate much less savings. Funds gained from reductions in military spending that are not used to reduce the federal deficit should be redirected to the nation's most serious domestic problems, of which poverty and its well-known corollaries are among the most important.

There are alternative means of raising federal revenues in a progressive and fair manner that would more than make up for the recommended added expenditures. One alternative is to raise the taxes of the affluent, who benefited most from the tax cuts of the 1980s. Congress should consider setting a higher bracket of 38 percent for individuals with the highest income, with the tax rate on the current highest bracket—which would become the second highest bracket—raised from 31 to 33 percent. Second, an increase of twenty-five cents per gallon in the gasoline tax would encourage conservation and discourage traffic congestion, as well as raise substantial revenue. Third, the current partial exemption of social security income from taxation primarily benefits elderly individuals who are better off. Keeping the current tax-free social security income thresholds of $25,000 for individuals and $32,000 for couples would protect those will less income, but the excess amount of social security income subject to taxation should be increased from 50 to 85 percent. Finally, the mortgage interest income deduction should be limited for those with expensive or multiple homes. These tax proposals would generate more than $200 billion over a five-year period, and some of the amount not used to reduce the budget deficit should be invested in antipoverty programs.[6]

The increased costs necessary to assist the working poor should also be weighed against the costs of inaction. In the past few years, the federal government has reduced its role in promoting tight labor markets and assisting the working poor. The costs have been higher unemployment, more poverty, added deprivation, and greater dependency on government.

Which Path Will Be Followed?

Free market ideology has strong political support and mitigates against the adoption of more effective worker protections, and the large federal budget deficit makes the expansion of almost all programs difficult. Politicians are reluctant to raise taxes or re-duce tax expenditures, even if the burden falls on the rich.

Support for federal intervention tends to be cyclical. Retrench-ments in the early 1980s reflected, in part, disgruntlement with the less than dramatic effects of stepped-up federal efforts to com-bat poverty. Indeed, the problems of the poor are frequently intrac-table, but many government programs have been more successful than is generally known or believed. The Job Corps has assisted disadvantaged teenagers who would have remained among the hard-core unemployed. Cash assistance has alleviated depriva-tion; food stamps and Medicaid have improved diets and health care. If these successes are made known, and the problems of the poor continue, political pressure might shift in favor of stronger federal programs. In fact, opinion polls indicate that although the public remains skeptical about the effectiveness of government efforts, the majority of the population supports increased spending on poverty programs, especially in the areas of education, training, and job creation. Notwithstanding the changes of recent years, the structure of antipoverty programs remains intact. An entirely new system does not need to be constructed; much can be accomplished if the old system is repaired.

As a group, the working poor are well positioned to benefit from renewed public support of affirmative government action. They do try to help themselves, but they are often defeated in surmounting the obstacles they face in their struggles for economic self-sufficiency. The millions of working poor confound the long-ingrained belief and hope prevalent in this nation that work leads to an adequate if not prosperous life. Their existence undermines the truism that a commitment to the work ethic provides a road out of poverty.

Targeted federal government policies are only one funding source addressed to reducing the persistence of work and poverty. State and local governments, the private sector, and other institutions should all act together to diminish poverty among workers. Of course, impoverished individuals also need to recognize their responsibilities for achieving self-sufficiency. A positive and active role for the federal government is a crucial element in adequately addressing the difficulties of this nation's needy citizens. That element should be restored.

Notes

2. Profile of the Working Poor

1. U.S. Congress, House of Representatives, Committee on Ways and Means, *1992 Green Book: Background Material and Data on Programs within the Jurisdiction of the Committee on Ways and Means,* May 15, 1992, p. 1282.

2. Rebecca M. Blank, "Growth Is Not Enough: Why the Recovery of the 1980's Did So Little to Reduce Poverty?" U.S. Congress, Joint Economic Committee, September 26, 1991.

3. Center for Labor Market Studies and Center for Applied Social Research, *Social and Economic Indicators for the Nation's Family Households* (New York: Russell Sage Foundation, 1990), vol. 2, table 4E12.

4. William O'Hare et al., *Real Life Poverty in America: Where the American Public Would Set the Poverty Line* (Washington: Center on Budget and Policy Priorities and Families USA Foundation, July 1990); and Patricia Ruggles, *Drawing the Line: Alternative Poverty Measures and Their Implications for Public Policy* (Washington: Urban Institute Press, 1990).

5. Kathleen Short and Martina Shea, *Transitions in Income and Poverty Status: 1987–1988* (Washington: Government Printing Office, August 1991), Census Bureau Household Economic Studies, Series P-70, No. 24, pp. 50–51.

6. Mary Jo Bane and David T. Ellwood, "Slipping Into and Out of Poverty: The Dynamics of Spells," *Journal of Human Resources* (Winter 1986): 19.

7. Richard B. Freeman, "Troubled Workers in the Labor Market," *Seventh Annual Report: The Federal Interest in Employment and Training* (Washington: National Commission for Employment Policy, October 1981), pp. 106, 112, 115.

3. Low-Wage Job Markets

1. Unpublished tabulations of the Current Population Survey by Andrew Sum, Northeastern University, and Robert Taggart, Remediation and Training Institute.

2. Paul Ryscavage and Peter Henle, "Earnings Inequality in the 1980s," *Monthly Labor Review* (December 1990): 3–16.

3. John McNeil, *Workers with Low Earnings: 1964 to 1990* (Washington: Government Printing Office, March 1992), Census Bureau Current Publication Report, Series P-60, No. 178, p. 3, plus unpublished data.

4. McKinley Blackburn, Richard Freeman, and David Bloom, "Changes in Earnings Differentials in the 1980s: Concordance, Convergence, Causes, and Consequences," National Bureau of Economic Research, Cambridge, Mass., Working Paper No. 3901, November 1991.

5. Michael Abramowitz, "The Urban Boom: Who Benefits?" *Washington Post,* May 10, 1992, p. H1.

6. National Center on Education and the Economy, *America's Choice: High Skills or Low Wages?* (Rochester, N.Y.: National Center, June 1990).

7. Richard Cyert and David Mowery, *Technology and Employment* (Washington: National Academy Press, 1987), pp. 20–21, 31, 99.

8. Cited in Edward F. Dement, *Out of Sight, Out of Mind* (Washington: National Governors' Association, August 1985), p. 4.

9. U.S. General Accounting Office, *Hired Farmworkers: Health and Well-Being at Risk* (Washington: GAO, February 1992), HRD-92-46, p. 26.

10. U.S. Bureau of International Labor Affairs, *Employer Sanctions and U.S. Labor Markets* (Washington: Labor Department, July 1991), p. 3 (updated).

11. U.S. General Accounting Office, *Illegal Aliens: Influence of Illegal Workers on Wages and Working Conditions of Legal Workers* (Washington: GAO, March 1988), p. 1; and U.S. Bureau of International Labor Affairs, "The Effects of Immigration on the U.S. Economy and Labor Market," in *Immigration Policy and Research Report* (Washington: Labor Department, May 1989), pp. 180–84.

4. Making Work Pay

1. Bruce Klein, "Real Estimates of Poor Minimum Wage Workers," *Challenge* (May/June 1992): 53–55.

2. *Report of the Minimum Wage Study Commission* (Washington: Government Printing Office, 1981), vol. 1, p. 156.

3. Statement of Representative George Miller, in *The Reemergence of Sweatshops and the Enforcement of Wage and Hour Standards of the Committee on Education and Labor,* U.S. House of Representatives, 97th Cong., 1st and 2d sess. (Washington: Government Printing Office, 1982), p. 4.

4. U.S. General Accounting Office, *Sweatshops in the U.S.: Opinions on Their Extent and Possible Enforcement Options* (Washington: GAO, August 1988).

5. *Report of the Minimum Wage Study Commission,* p. 38.

6. Alison Wellington, "Effects of the Minimum Wage on the Employment Status of Youths: An Update," *Journal of Human Resources* (Winter 1991): 27–46.

7. David Card, Princeton University, "Using Regional Variation in Wages to Measure the Effects of the Federal Minimum Wage," Draft Paper presented at Cornell University Conference on New Minimum Wage Research, November 15, 1991; and Lawrence Katz (Harvard University) and Alan B. Krueger (Princeton University), "The Effects of the Minimum Wage on the Fast Food Industry," National Bureau of Economic Research, Cambridge, Mass., Working Paper No. 4058, April 1992.

8. David Card, "Do Minimum Wages Reduce Employment? A Case Study of California, 1987–89," Princeton University, Department of Economics, May 1991.

9. Katz and Krueger, "The Effect of the Minimum Wage on the Fast Food Industry."

10. Much of this EITC discussion is drawn from Robert Greenstein and Isaac Shapiro, "Policies to Alleviate Rural Poverty," in *Rural Poverty in America,* ed. Cynthia Duncan (New York: Auburn House, 1992).

11. U.S. General Accounting Office, *Earned Income Tax Credit: Advance Payment Option Is Not Widely Known or Understood by the Public* (Washington: GAO, February 1992).

12. U.S. Congress, House of Representatives, Committee on Ways and Means, *1992 Green Book: Background Material and Data on Programs within the Jurisdiction of the Committee on Ways and Means,* May 15, 1992, p. 1527.

5. Removing Employment Obstacles

1. Unpublished tabulations from the March 1991 Current Population Survey, provided by Andrew Sum, Northeastern University (data exclude school enrollees).

2. Stephen Cameron and James Heckman, "The Nonequivalence of High School Equivalents," University of Chicago Economics Department, June 1991.

3. Sar Levitan and Frank Gallo, *Got to Learn to Earn: Preparing Americans for Work* (Washington: George Washington University Center for Social Policy Studies, September 1991), pp. 19–22.

4. U.S. National Center for Education Statistics, "Adult Education Profile for 1990–91," Statistics in Brief NCES 91-222, September 1991, p. 6.

5. Sar Levitan and Frank Gallo, "Uncle Sam's Helping Hand: Educating, Training, and Employing the Disadvantaged," in *New Developments*

in Worker Training: A Legacy for the 1990s, ed. Louis Ferman et al. (Madison, Wis.: Industrial Relations Research Association, 1990), p. 244.

6. Howard Bloom et al., *The National JTPA Study: Title IIA Impacts on Earnings and Employment at Eighteen Months, Executive Summary* (Bethesda, Md.: Abt Associates, May 1992), p. 4.

7. Sar A. Levitan, *Evaluation of Federal Social Programs* (Washington: Center for Social Policy Studies, June 1992), pp. 23–24.

8. U.S. General Accounting Office, *Vocational Rehabilitation Program: Client Characteristics, Services Received, and Employment Outcomes* (Washington: GAO, November 12, 1991), T-PEMD-92-3, pp. 3–4.

9. June O'Neill, "Women and Wages," *American Enterprise* (November/December 1990): 25–33.

10. Margery Austin Turner, Michael Fix, and Raymond Struyk, *Opportunities Denied, Opportunities Diminished: Discrimination in Hiring* (Washington: Urban Institute, 1991), pp. 9–10, 14, 19, 29.

11. Jonathan Leonard, "The Federal Anti-Bias Effort," in *Essays on the Economics of Discrimination,* ed. Emily Hoffman (Kalamazoo, Mich.: W. E. Upjohn Institute for Employment Research, 1991), pp. 85–113.

12. Peter Cattan, "Child Care Problems: An Obstacle to Work," *Monthly Labor Review* (October 1991): 3–9.

6. Finding and Creating Jobs

1. U.S. General Accounting Office, *Employment Service: Improved Leadership Needed for Better Performance* (Washington: GAO, August 1991), HRD-91-88, p. 36.

2. Terry Johnson et al., *National Evaluation of the Impact of the United States Employment Service* (Menlo Park, Calif.: SRI International, June 1983).

3. Joseph Ball et al., *The Participation of Private Businesses as Work Sponsors in the Youth Entitlement Demonstration* (New York: Manpower Demonstration Research Corp., March 1981), pp. 6–7, 33–34.

4. U.S. General Accounting Office, *Targeted Jobs Tax Credit: Employer Actions to Recruit, Hire, and Retain Eligible Workers Vary* (Washington: GAO, February 1991), HRD-91-33, p. 15.

5. Sar A. Levitan and Elizabeth I. Miller, *Federal Assistance to Indian Reservations* (Washington: George Washington University Center for Social Policy Studies, 1992).

6. Sar Levitan and Frank Gallo, *Spending to Save: Expanding Employment Opportunities* (Washington: George Washington University Center for Social Policy Studies, February 1992).

7. U.S. General Accounting Office, *Strong Internal Controls at Service Delivery Level Will Help Prevent CETA-Type Fraud and Abuse in Job Training Partnership Act Programs* (Washington: GAO, September 28, 1984).

8. Robert Cook et al., *Public Service Employment in Fiscal 1980*

(Princeton, N.J.: Woodrow Wilson School of Public and International Affairs, March 1981), pp. 29–30.

7. Linking Welfare with Work

1. U.S. General Accounting Office, *Food Stamp Program: A Demographic Analysis of Participation and Nonparticipation* (Washington: GAO, January 1990), PEMD-90-8, pp. 11, 16, 41; and U.S. Congress, House of Representatives, Committee on Ways and Means, *1991 Green Book: Background Material and Data on Programs within the Jurisdiction of the Committee on Ways and Means,* 1991, p. 1400.

2. Richard Kronick, "Health Insurance, 1979–1989: The Frayed Connection between Employment and Insurance," *Inquiry* (Winter 1991): 318–32.

3. U.S. General Accounting Office, *Medicaid Expansions: Coverage Improves but State Fiscal Problems Jeopardize Continued Progress* (Washington: GAO, June 1991), HRD-91-78, pp. 13, 29–37.

4. U.S. Bureau of Labor Statistics, *Consumer Expenditure Survey, 1988–89* (Washington: Government Printing Office, August 1991), pp. 99–122.

5. Edward Lazere, Cushing Dolbeare, Paul Leonard, and Barry Zigas, *A Place to Call Home* (Washington: Center on Budget and Policy Priorities, and Low Income Housing Information Service, December 1991), p. 5.

6. Ibid., pp. 27, 32.

7. David Bloom and Richard Freeman, "The Fall in Private Pension Coverage in the U.S.," Columbia University Economic Discussion Paper No. 576, January 1992, pp. 1, 3, 12.

8. Sar Levitan and Frank Gallo, "Work and Family: The Impact of Legislation," *Monthly Labor Review* (March 1990): 34–40.

9. Isaac Shapiro and Marion Nichols, *Far from Fixed: An Analysis of the Unemployment Insurance System* (Washington: Center on Budget and Policy Priorities, March 1992), p. 1; and Gene Falk, *The Uncompensated Unemployed: An Analysis of Unemployed Workers Who Do Not Receive Unemployment Compensation* (Washington: U.S. Congressional Research Service, November 15, 1990), 90-565 EPW, p. 28.

10. Ralph Smith and Bruce Vavrichek, *Family Incomes of Unemployment Insurance Recipients and the Implications for Extending Benefits* (Washington: U.S. Congressional Budget Office, February 1990), pp. 28–31.

11. U.S. Census Bureau, *Measuring the Effect of Benefits and Taxes on Income and Poverty: 1990* (Washington: Government Printing Office, August 1991), Current Population Report, P-60, No. 176-RD, pp. 40–41, 64–67.

12. Sar Levitan, *Programs in Aid of the Poor,* 6th ed. (Baltimore: Johns Hopkins University Press, 1990), pp. 49–51.

13. Michael Puma, Nancy Burstein, Katie Merrell, and Gary Sil-

verstein, *Evaluation of the Food Stamp Employment and Training Program: Final Report* (Alexandria, Va.: U.S. Food and Nutrition Service, June 1990), pp. xiii, x–xii.

14. U.S. General Accounting Office, *Welfare to Work: States Begin JOBS, but Fiscal and Other Problems May Impede Their Progress* (Washington: GAO, September 1991), HRD-91-106.

15. James Riccio and Daniel Friedlander, *GAIN: Program Strategies, Participation Patterns, and First-Year Impacts in Six Counties* (New York: Manpower Demonstration Research Corporation, May 1992), pp. x–xi.

16. Jan Hagen and Irene Lurie, *Implementing JOBS: Initial State Choices, Summary Report* (Albany: State University of New York, Nelson A. Rockefeller Institute of Government, March 1992), pp. 10–11, 15.

17. Isaac Shapiro et al., *The States and the Poor: How Budget Decisions in 1991 Affected Low Income People* (Washington: Center on Budget and Policy Priorities and Center for the Study of States, December 1991), pp. 21–23.

18. Lewin/ICF and James Bell Associates, *State and Local General Assistance Programs* (Washington: Lewin/ICF, November 1990), pp. 20, 23, 30–31, appendix B.

8. Looking Down the Road

1. Sar Levitan, Garth Mangum, and Stephen Mangum, *The Economics of Rectitude: Necessary but Not Sufficient* (Washington: George Washington University, Center for Social Policy Studies, 1992).

2. Sar Levitan and Elizabeth Miller, *Enterprise Zones: A Promise Based on Rhetoric* (Washington: George Washington University, Center for Social Policy Studies, March 1992).

3. "Opinion Outlook," *National Journal* (June 20, 1992): 1486.

4. Ibid.

5. Sar Levitan and Frank Gallo, *Got to Learn to Earn: Preparing Americans for Work* (Washington: George Washington University, Center for Social Policy Studies, September 1991), p. 50.

6. U.S. Congressional Budget Office, *Reducing the Deficit: Spending and Revenue Options* (Washington: Government Printing Office, February 1992), pp. 287, 294, 309, 340.

Index

Adult education programs, vii, 8, 68–69, 135
Affirmative action, 78, 134
Age Discrimination in Employment Act (1967), 78
Agriculture: employment in, 30, 31; federal subsidies, 136; migrant farm workers, 37–40
Aid to Families with Dependent Children (AFDC), 112–13, 128; benefit levels, 100–101, 102, 114; childcare subsidies, 10, 119, 121; duration of assistance, 100; and EITC payments, 60; eligibility restrictions, 101–2, 121; employment and training programs, 10, 85, 117, 120, 122, 123; funding for, 10–11, 100; health insurance coverage, 104, 105–6, 132; unemployed parent program, 101, 116–17; work disincentives of, 104, 116–17, 132; workfare requirements, 115–18, 119–20, 121, 123, 124–25
Americans with Disabilities Act (1990), 78, 79, 134
Antidiscrimination laws, 9, 77–80, 133–34
Appalachia, poverty in, 35
Area Redevelopment Act (1961), 69

Blacks: employment discrimination and, 76, 77, 134; employment obstacles of, 20; family size and earnings, 24; minimum-wage workers, 46; single-parent families, 22; unemployment rates, 75–76
Blue-collar occupations, 30–31, 34
Bush, George, 80–81, 91
Bush administration, 126; and employment tax credits, 90, 91; and equal employment opportunity, 78, 134; and minimum-wage reduction, 55

California: general assistance program, 123; Greater Avenues for Independence (GAIN), 121; immigration to, 40, 41; minimum wage, 53
Cash assistance, 10, 98, 132, 137; AFDC, 100; expenditure levels, 113, 123; poverty-reduction effects, 102; public resentment of, 115; state general assistance, 123
Childcare, vii, viii, 127, 133; as employment obstacle, 9, 19, 21, 24, 29, 64, 80; federal subsidies, 9, 80–82, 119; income-tax credits, 82; state programs, 10, 81, 121
Children, 61; AFDC benefits, 100, 123; divorce and, 131; educational attainment levels, 64, 65, 67–68; EITC benefits, 45, 57, 59–60;

training, 83; unemployment insurance taxes, 110

Employment: and AFDC eligibility, 116–17, 122; childcare barriers to, 9, 19, 21, 24, 29, 64, 80; educational barriers to, 8, 19–20; equal opportunity laws, viii-ix, 11, 64, 74, 82; minimum wage and, 51–54, 55–57, 130, 134; obstacles for the poor, 7, 9, 35, 82–83; and poverty rates, 15; private-sector employment, 123, 129, 133, 138; public-service jobs, 9–10, 93, 94–95, 123, 132; summer jobs program, 69, 91–92, 93; technological change and, 36; and welfare recipients, 98, 101–2, 113, 115; work disabilities, 8, 20; work ethic and, 6, 12, 51–52, 116, 127, 133, 138; work incentives and disincentives, 5–6, 99, 104, 124–25, 127–28. *See also* Employers; Labor markets; Occupations; Part-time work

Employment discrimination, 64, 74–77, 130; antidiscrimination laws, 9, 77–80, 133–34

Employment service, 9, 39, 84–88, 96, 133; employers and, 85, 86–87; and employment tax credits, 90; funding of, 85

Employment training, viii, 8–9, 11, 69–73, 126; for AFDC recipients, 10, 85, 117, 120, 122, 123; federal expenditures, 9, 38–39, 69, 70–71, 117–18; job-search training, 70, 71, 72, 118; on-the-job training, 70, 71, 72; skill-training programs, 19–20, 98, 135; state programs, 119, 120

English-as-a-second-language program, 68

Enterprise zones, 133

Equal Employment Opportunity Commission (EEOC), 78

Equal employment opportunity laws, viii-ix, 11, 64, 74, 82

Equal Pay Act (1963), 77

Even Start Family Literacy program, 81–82

Excise taxes, 57

Executive order 11246, 78

Fair Housing Act (1988), 80

Fair Labor Standards Act (1938), 7, 38, 45–46, 50

Families: AFDC recipients, 100–101; EITC benefits, 58–60, 61; employment barriers of, 21, 133; female-headed, 16, 18, 22–24; government assistance to, 26, 103, 116, 132; single-parent, viii, 9, 22, 25, 101, 117, 119, 131; size of, 22, 24–25, 48, 60; working poor, 15, 18, 19, 22, 131

Family Support Act (1988): AFDC-coverage requirements, 101, 105–6; childcare requirements, 9, 10; and child-support payments, 131; education and training requirements, 118, 121, 122

Fast-food industry, 55

Federal government policies, vii, viii, 6, 126–27; antidiscrimination laws, 9, 77–80, 133–34; childcare, 9, 10, 80–82, 121, 133; domestic problems, 126, 133, 136; education, 8–9, 67–68, 135; employment placement, 9, 84, 86, 87, 96; employment tax credits, 9, 84, 88; employment training, 9, 10, 69, 70–71, 117; equal employment opportunity, 11, 64, 74; housing assistance, 107; immigration, 39, 41, 129; job creation, 9–10, 84, 91, 93, 94, 96–97, 133; labor markets, 6, 9, 41–42; minimum wage, 7–8, 45–46, 134; public-works employment, 94–95; recommendations for, 127–37; social insurance, 107–8; taxation, 7, 8, 45, 82, 130–31, 136–37; vocational rehabilitation, 8, 73; welfare assistance, 10–11, 26, 100, 103, 111–16, 132; workfare, 117, 118–19, 130; and working poor,